QUARRY

Journey Journals, page 66

GLOUCESTER MASSACHUSETTS

Making Family Journals

Projects and Ideas for Sharing and Recording Memories Together

QUARRY BOOKS

Linda Blinn

First published in the United States of America by
Quarry Books, a member of
Quayside Publishing Group
33 Commercial Street
Gloucester, Massachusetts 01930-5089
Telephone: (978) 282-9590
Fax: (978) 283-2742
www.rockpub.com

Library of Congress Cataloging-in-Publication Data
Blinn, Linda.
  Making family journals : projects and ideas for sharing and recording memories together /
Linda Blinn.
      p.   cm.
  ISBN 1-59253-228-4 (pbk.)
  1. Handicraft. 2. Photograph albums. 3. Scrapbooks. 4. Family—Miscellanea. I. Title.
TT157.B6175 2006
  808.88'3—dc22   2005030263
                                                                                       CIP

ISBN-13: 978-1-59253-228-5
ISBN-10: 1-59253-228-4

10 9 8 7 6 5 4 3 2

Design: Yee Design
Cover Image: All photos by Allan Penn

Printed in Singapore

CASSIE GISSEL LAUREN ALLIE DYLAN LAN ZACH ANDREW

It was so much fun for the children to spend day in and day out with cousins!

Cassie got really into all the stickers and was fascinated with "Rub-ons" She did this page with all her cousins names on it.

La Familia, South of the Border, *page 60*

Contents

Italian Journal, page 56

Home is Where the Art Is, page 72

Italian Journal, page 56

Introduction

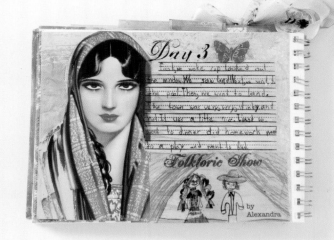

Journey Journal, page 66

JOIN A LIVELY GROUP OF ARTISTS and their families on an artistic journey from places far away to home sweet home. In this book you'll explore the ways that different families artfully depict life's passages with journaling, photography, scrapbooking, and memory art. Our definition of family is broad and goes beyond relatives to include the social families with whom we play, travel, cook, work, and celebrate.

The how-to projects in this book were designed by artists, designers, moms, authors, and teachers with expertise in a broad range of mixed-media art. The focus of the book is directed toward activities appealing to family members from toddlers to adults. Workshop instructor Traci Bautista generously shares the innovative bookbinding techniques she developed specifically for children. Ruth Giauque and other artistic mothers offer clear and concise instructions for the books, journals, and projects they have designed to celebrate and commemorate family life.

The travel chapter reveals examples of amazing ingenuity and imagination; both are requirements for *art on the road.* A group of home-school families organized an educational trip to Tuscany where they lived on a farm and studied bookmaking and art. While there, Jill Littlewood restored a 150-year-old ledger and filled it with rubbings, transfers, and sketches she made on the trip.

Christine and Erik Adolph—both accomplished artists and designers—traveled to Mexico with their daughters. When they returned to the cruise ship each evening, they spread their cache of ephemera and found objects on the beds and created journals bursting with colors, sketches, and observations.

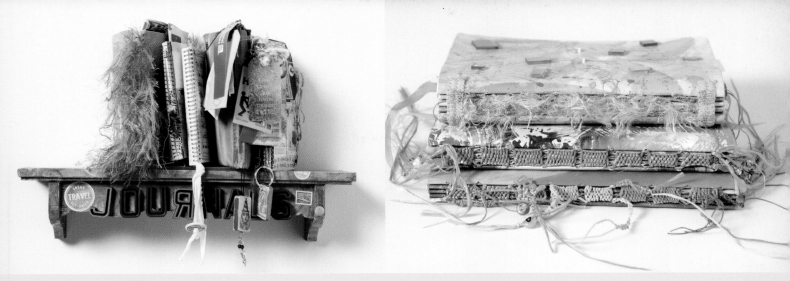

Journey Journals, page 66

Child's Play, page 42

On the home front, Jenn Mason's hunky, chunky house book—with its binding made from materials found at the hardware store—looks back at former residences and chronicles the important events that happened at each address. With photography, journaling, and artwork contributed by her husband and her daughters, the book offers an example of an ongoing family project that is both approachable and enjoyable.

My dream cottage is depicted in a three-dimensional model with tiny books spilling out of every door. I glued together three balsa-wood houses found at a craft store and enlisted my husband Tom to build a miniature copper pergola for the cottage. (Tom secretly hopes he never has to actually *live* in a pink and ochre house.)

These chapters are organized in a timeline from the future to present to the past. When dreams and desires turn your focus forward, Suzee Gallagher's eye-catching, dream-catching book made from large envelopes will be just the project to accommodate your family's wish lists. While in present time, easy bookbinding directions will convince you that you can make a book. *Right now!*

Remembering, reflecting, and researching are themes for the past. In the family history chapters, exploring resources for researching your genealogy may become your favorite *pastime* activity. Regardless of which time period inspires you to start a family project, *any* time spent creating together is as significant as the events you choose to document.

—Linda Blinn

CHAPTER I

Making Books Easy:

Simple Structures, Personalization, and Embellishment

ARE YOU MORE COMFORTABLE WITH A GLUE STICK OR A SEWING machine? An awl or a computer? Do precise cuts make your heart sing or give you the whim whams? Are you drawn to things vintage or those that are refined and minimal? Do you like the challenge of experimenting with new techniques, tools, and styles? Or have you found your niche, knowing exactly what projects you like and are comfortable with? All these issues are considered in the scope of projects offered in this chapter.

If you are already adept at making handmade books or have amassed a collection of purchased blank journals, perhaps the ideas for embellishments, tab dividers, or page edges will be just what you need to personalize those books. No matter where or how you start, the ultimate goal for making family journals is to reflect your creativity, your style, and your very special family.

Putting Together a Basic Tool Kit

Most of the projects in this book can be put together with easy-to-find materials. There are a few basic items that you will use repeatedly to make various projects. Assemble the following items and consider it your basic kit. You will find this kit as part of each project's Materials list throughout the book.

BASIC TOOL KIT:

- pencil
- PVA glue
- spray adhesive
- glue stick
- double-sided tape
- bone folder
- craft knife
- scissors
- cutting mat
- metal ruler

FIVE WAYS TO EXPAND YOUR DESIGN SKILLS

- **DIMINISH** *the fear factor by using old magazine pages for paper when you are experimenting with new techniques.*

- **CONSIDER** *many different sizes, shapes, and materials. Don't rule out anything until you try it.*

- **USE** *what you have on hand—it makes you think more creatively.*

- **DESIGNATE** *an area to keep the supplies and materials so they can be used even if you just have a few minutes to experiment or play.*

- **MOCK UP** *the book first with plain paper—by the time you start the actual project, you will understand the steps.*

Child's Play, page 42

The Pamphlet Stitch

This binding method is simple, versatile, and quick. Like any classic, it allows unlimited opportunities to experiment with unconventional materials such as ball chain, rubber bands, or even shoelaces. When working with children (or husbands), precise cutting and perfectly aligned corners are not as important as the charm and personality that comes from imperfection. The message: Lighten up! Anyone who can fold paper, punch a hole, and tie a knot has all the necessary skills.

MATERIALS

- various papers for pages
- heavy stock for the cover
- tapestry needle
- awl
- heavy thread
- basic tool kit

Three-Hole Pamphlet Stitch with a Tie on the Outside

To begin, fold four pieces of same-sized paper in half. Smooth the folds down from the center to the edge. Nest all the sheets together. Make three pencil marks: one in the center of the fold, and one approximately 1" (2.5 cm) from the top and another approximately 1" (2.5 cm) from the bottom. Now you are ready to sew the pamphlet stitch.

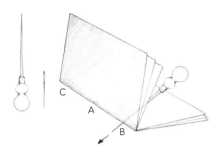

1. With a tapestry needle or awl, pierce three holes starting from the innermost fold and push through the outermost fold.

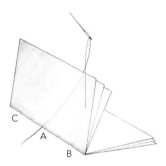

2. Cut a piece of thread measuring three times the length of the fold. Thread the needle (no knot necessary), and stitch as follows: Starting on the outside, insert the needle through the center hole (A), leaving a 3" (7.6 cm) length on the outside.

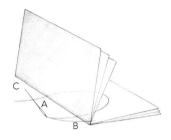

3. Take the needle through hole B from the inside to the outside.

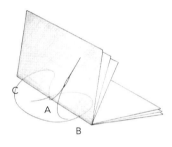

4. Guide the needle in through hole C from the outside, then from the inside go back through hole A to the outside.

5. Pull taut, and tie a knot with a bow. **NOTE:** The binding can also be reversed to end inside the book instead of outside.

Five and Seven Hole Pamphlet Stitch for Larger Books

This bookbinding method adapts to the size of your book—from mini to large—just increase or decrease the number of holes. Remember to use odd numbers—3, 5, 7, 9, 11—so you will always have a middle hole. To begin, mark holes for the center and 1" (2.5 cm) from each end. The remaining pairs of holes should be equidistant from the center.

1. After boring holes, take the needle from the inside to the outside of the center hole, then back through the adjacent hole above.

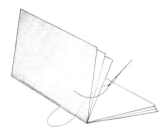

4. Skip the center hole, and go out through the hole below it.

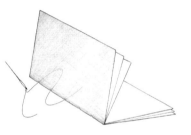

2. Bring the needle out through the end hole at the top.

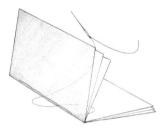

5. Go back in through the bottom hole.

3. Go back in through the second hole from the top (so you are moving back down the spine).

6. Go out through the adjacent hole above, and back in the center hole. Pull taut and tie a knot.

Simple Book Cover

A wrapper cover can be sewn on as you stitch the pamphlet or simply tucked in with the first and last pages of the book. Use heavier paper for the cover.

1. Measure and cut the cover so it is the same height and four times the width of the pages.

2. Fold the cover paper in half.

3. Place the spine of the pamphlet book against the center fold of the cover page.

4. Mark where the foredge of the pages hit the cover.

5. Fold at the marks made in step 4 to create the flaps, folding toward the spine.

6. Bore holes in the cover to match the hole in the pages, then stitch together.

For a non-sewn version of this cover, follow steps 1–5 and then simply tuck the flaps around the first and last pages of the book.

VARIATIONS AND EMBELLISHMENTS FOR SIMPLE BOOK COVERS

- *To insert a ribbon tie, make a slice on the fold, insert the ribbon, and secure it with double-sided tape on the inside.*

- *Cut out a square or other shape in the center of the cover to frame an image.*

- *Tear the page edges, then line them with metallic pen.*

- *Create a series of pamphlet books with a theme.*

- *Slide beads onto the binding ties and secure them with a knot.*

- *Include tabs and tuck-ins.*

PAPER CHOICES

Combine different colors, sizes, and types of paper. For example, for the pages you could use crinkled kraft paper, handmade papers, paste papers, parchment paper, scrapbook paper, recycled paper from old ledgers, or old documents. For the cover, you could use watercolor paper, cardstock, corrugated paper, laminated paper or fabric, anaglyptic wallpaper, canvas, heavy fabric with iron-on backing, or handmade and decorated papers.

BINDING MATERIALS

Try embroidery thread, linen thread, elastic, twine, cord, fabric tape, small metal ball chain, rubber band, vines, or safety pins.

Instant Vintage Journal

Transform a purchased journal by adhering canvas photocopies of artwork from vintage books. The New York Public Library Digital Collection—where you can find a collection of 2,509 book jackets—is a valuable resource for this project. The playful image on the cover of this book was downloaded from their website. It's fine to use these images for your personal artwork. For other purposes, request permission from the Library's Photographic Services and Permissions office.

BELOW: *The key to converting purchased canvas journals into books with character is to incorporate copies of old book parts. This is done by photocopying spines and covers of old books on to a special canvas made for printers. The canvas is then glued to the surface of the new journals. Is it old or new? These techniques will make it hard to tell the difference.*

- purchased blank journal with canvas cover (any size)
- printable canvas (available at craft and office supply stores)
- used book
- decorative paper
- photocopies of vintage endpapers from other books
- ribbon
- embellishments
- gesso
- clear acrylic spray to seal the surface
- basic tool kit

"This is a quick and easy project geared toward teens and adults. Hunting for vintage books with interesting covers becomes addictive!"

Designing the Cover

1. Make a colored photocopy of the cover of an old book or print an image from the New York Public Library Digital Collection. (See page 104 for details).

2. Adjust the size so it is approximately the size of the cover—it does not need to be exact.

3. Copy the image on to the printable canvas.

4. Affix the canvas to the front of the book with spray adhesive.

5. Trim the edges to fit the cover (do not wrap the canvas around the edge).

6. Embellish other surfaces of the book cover, such as the spine, with decorative paper or collage items.

Making the Ribbon Tie

1. Open the journal and mark the center of the edge of the front and back cover.

2. Cut two pieces of ribbon, each measuring 6" (15.2 cm) long.

3. Using the center mark as a guide, glue $1^1/_2$" (3.8 cm) of the ribbon to the inside of the front cover. Repeat for the back cover. NOTE: If you want the ribbon to be flush with the surface, use a sharp craft knife and cut a shallow channel in the cover $1^1/_2$" (3.8 cm) long, as wide as your ribbon, and approximately $1/_8$" (3 mm) deep. Glue the ribbon securely inside the channels.

Finishing the Book

1. Glue decorative paper to the inside covers of your journal to serve as endpapers.

2. Add envelopes and library pockets to the inside covers.

3. Lightly dry brush gesso over all surfaces to give the book a cohesive look.

4. Spray the outside covers with clear acrylic coating to seal.

Machine-Stitched Memory Book

One straight line of machine stitching holds this colorful book together while creating channels in which to place swizzle sticks, colored pencils, knitting needles, chopsticks, or twigs. Ribbons and decorative paper carry out the theme while the accordion pullout provides extra space for photos, envelopes, journaling, or artwork. Creating one of these books every holiday season will result in a fine collection commemorating years of family gatherings. For another variation, create an art book by filling the pages with children's artwork reduced in size on a copier. Place paintbrushes in the channels to accent the theme.

NOTE: While you have the sewing machine set up, make multiple copies of this versatile book to keep on hand. When you need a special gift, this book can quickly be personalized and embellished.

ABOVE: *Commemorate a vacation, holiday gathering, or your nature walks in this quick and easy book.*

- 5 sheets of double-sided cardstock in different colors (Prism)
- decorative paper
- ribbon
- plastic swizzle sticks
- bulldog clip
- sewing machine
- basic tool kit

Preparing the Basic Book

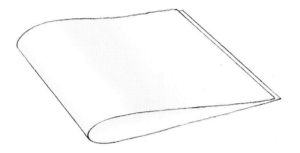

1. Cut all five sheets of paper to measure 6" x 12" (15.2 x 30.5 cm).

2. Fold each sheet in half and stack the sheets in the color sequence of your choice. Align and clamp them together at the top with a bulldog clip. Make a light pencil line from top to bottom on the left (spine) side, $1/2$" (1.3 cm) from the folded edge. Machine stitch on the pencil line.

"Once this book has been sewn together, children can participate in decorating the pages and covers."

Making the Accordion Insert

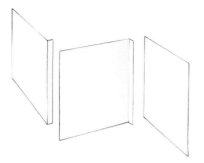

1. From the remaining pieces of cardstock, cut two pieces measuring 6" x $6^{1}/2$" (15.2 x 16.5 cm). Cut one piece measuring 6" x 6" (15.2 x 15.2 cm).

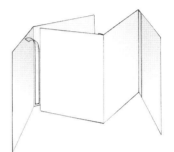

2. Fold a $1/2$" (1.3 cm) hinge on the end of each 6" x $6^{1}/2$" (15.2 x 16.5 cm) piece. Using the illustration for reference, glue or machine stitch the hinges to the adjacent pages to make the accordion fold out.

3. Affix the accordion fold out to the inside of the back cover with double-sided tape.

Making the Embellishments

1. With shears, cut the ball end off of plastic swizzle sticks.

2. Insert swizzle sticks into the channel of the front and back pages.

3. Insert ribbons through remaining channels, leaving a 3" (7.6 cm) tail at the top and bottom.

4. Affix squares of decorative papers to the front and back covers with a glue stick.

Shabby Chic Slipcovered Book

If a fabric slipcover can transform a sofa, imagine what it can do for an old hardcover book. This project is as easy as making a pillowcase and it is a great way to recycle old books and fabric. Consider padding the covers for a plush, cushy look. The pages are made from a variety of colored and vintage papers. Warning: If you are reluctant to tear all the pages out of an old book, this project is not for you. However, you may get past that problem when you see the results of recycling the book's cover into a useful and attractive journal. (And you can always put those old pages to work in collages.)

NOTE: When making more than one book at a time, set up an assembly line and assign tasks to your helpers according to age and skill level.

"A matching set of three books, each with a different bow, would make a gorgeous gift."

RIGHT: *Vintage fabric, flea-market table linens, and outgrown baby clothes are some of the possible covers for this one-of-a-kind book.*

MATERIALS

- used book with a ¹/₂" (1.3 cm) spine
- fabric
- iron-on tape or fusible webbing
- file folder
- various papers for pages
- sewing machine
- ribbon
- basic tool kit

Creating the Slipcover

1. Remove the pages from the old book using a craft knife.

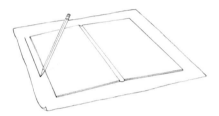

2. Lay the open book on fabric. Mark a line on the fabric 1¹/₂" (1.3 cm) from the book's edges. Cut two pieces of fabric to this size. Pin the right sides of the fabric together (facing each other).

3. Machine stitch three sides, leaving one short end open. Turn the fabric right side out. Press the seam and corners.

4. Cut a piece of iron-on tape or fusible webbing the length of the fabric from top to bottom. Place the iron-on tape in the center (vertically) of the fabric that will be the inside of the cover, and adhere it with an iron according to the manufacturer's instructions.

5. Cut a slit in the center of the tape or webbing, stopping ¹/₂" (1.3 cm) from the top and bottom.

Creating the Pages

1. Cut 6 to 8 pages ¹/₄" (6 mm) smaller than the cover on all sides.

2. Fold the pages in half, nest them together, and machine stitch down the center.

3. Cut a letter-size file folder approximately 1" (2.5 cm) smaller than the paper on all sides. Do not cut the fold.

4. Machine stitch the center of the paper to the center of the open file folder, keeping all sides equidistant.

5. Flip all the pages over to the right side and insert the left side of file folder into the slit in the tape or webbing on the inside of the cover. Repeat for the right side. Add a bow if desired.

Page Decor: Edges and Tab Dividers

EDGES

Whether the style of your book is elegant or funky, giving the page edges a bit of added detail, color, or texture can actually transform the look of the entire book. Not every page needs to be decorated. The first page of each section or chapter might be highlighted with decorative edges or a clever tab—or both. Coordinate the color and theme of the book with the edging to establish a feeling of continuity.

MATERIALS

- small-scale print fabric
- bleach
- roller stamp
- acrylic paint
- old credit card
- foil
- foil glue
- double-sided tape
- stencils
- rubber stamps
- rubber stamp pads

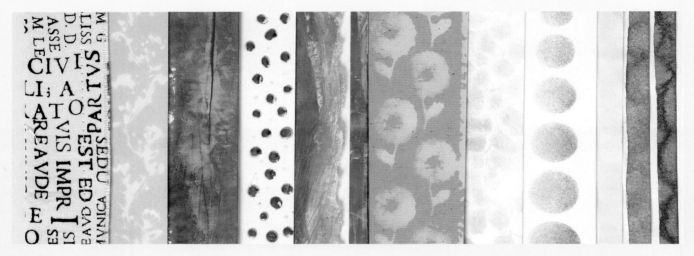

FROM LEFT TO RIGHT

1. **Stitched fabric.** Tear or cut fabric the length of the page and machine stitch it to the edge.

2. **Bleach-out technique using a roller stamp.** Pour a small amount of bleach into a shallow container such as a disposable aluminum pan. Run the roller stamp through the bleach so that the entire wheel is coated. Roll the stamp along the edge of the page.

3. **Acrylic paint.** Place two of three drops of acrylic paint at the top of the page. With the edge of a credit card, pull the paint to the bottom edge in one motion.

4. **Foil dots.** Using the tip on a foil glue container, make various size dots down the edge. Let dry. Press various colors of foil onto the glue and rub.

5. **Metallic paint.** Apply acrylic paint and then dry brush with metallic gold paint. Trim the edge with decorative scissors.

6. **Foil strip.** Apply double-sided tape along the edge, leaving some of the width to wrap around to the other side. Place foil on top of the tape and burnish. Repeat on the other side.

7. **Bleach out stamp.** Choose a stamp with a chunky motif without too much detail. Apply bleach to the stamp with a foam applicator. Press it onto paper and lift it up immediately. Rinse the stamp.

8. **Stencil.** Use a stippling brush to apply ink from a stamp pad to a plastic or metal stencil. Small-scale designs work best on page edges.

9. **Stencil.** Follow the same technique as above using a circle template.

10. **Gradated colors.** Mix a thin solution of acrylic paint and water. Pour the paint into a container that is longer than the edge of the paper. The three samples displayed here show a color gradation based of the number of times the paper was dipped into the solution. This technique can be used with plain water for a ruffled edge. The paint or water should be between $1/2$" (1.3 cm) and 1" (2.5 cm) deep.

TAB DIVIDERS

Tab dividers are used to define sections of the book and add lively accents to punch up your theme. For "fast tabs," choose stickers, postage stamps, labels, or embellishments with an adhesive back. Another option is to turn decorative papers, text, or clip art images into tabs using double-sided tape.

NOTE: Small sections of maps make excellent tab dividers because they have printing on both sides.

MATERIALS

- epoxy stickers
- stamps
- labels
- text
- clip art images
- rub-on numbers or letters
- double-sided adhesive sheets (Peel n' Stick)
- clear contact paper

1. Apply double-sided adhesive backing to the tab if needed.

2. Place the adhesive backing on the side of the paper you have chosen for the back of your tab. The back can be a solid-color paper, decorative paper, or the same material as the front. Burnish and trim the edges of the tab.

3. Wrap the entire tab with clear contact paper, leaving a $1/4$" (6 mm) edge on the left side of the tab.

4. Separate the $1/4$" (6 mm) border of contact paper with the tip of a craft knife and adhere one edge of the contact paper to the front of the page, and the other side to the back of the page.

CHAPTER II

Visions of Tomorrow:
Wishes, Dreams, and Desires

WE ALL HAVE WISHES AND DREAMS; GENERALLY THEY STAY IN our heads. The process of moving from simply thinking about dreams to actually expressing them often leads to a lively family activity. Identifying your dreams is enlightening and may even be the first step in making them come true.

Further detailing your dreams and desires in books, journals, and family projects may recapture forgotten longings as well as help you look to the future. Believing that their dreams can become a reality is a powerful source of self-esteem for children. In her book *Wish It, Dream It, Do It,* author Leslie Levine states that dreaming is always age-appropriate. Small children don't need to be logical; let them have outrageous fantasies.

In this chapter, we show how the expression of family dreams and desires leads to exploration and creativity. The Strine family now anticipates the year 2020 when they can open the time capsule they filled with wish lists and predictions for the future. Suzee Gallagher uses her love of photography to show the contemplative nature of parental dreams for their children. And Linda Blinn turns savored images of the French countryside into a three-dimensional dream house project.

FIVE WAYS TO ENHANCE YOUR CREATIVITY

- **FANTASIZE** *as a way to dream big without putting parameters on what you really want.*

- **CONCEPTUALIZE** *your dreams as art; ask yourself why you want to acquire or do certain things. Write down the reasons.*

- **VERBALIZE** *what you want. If there is a word for it, you can ask for it, think about it, and share it.*

- **VISUALIZE** *your dream. What does it look like? What form does it take?*

- **REALIZE** *your dreams by assembling pictures, photographs, quotes, and phrases.*

Breathe, page 38

Time Capsule

ARTISTS: *The Strine Family—Lloyd, Allison, Olivia, and Drew*

As a seventh grader in 1972, Allison Strine participated in an unforgettable school project, creating a time capsule to be opened in the year 2000. She clearly remembers the thrill of making and packing precious items and imagining with wonder if the year 2000 would ever come. She actually called the school thirty years later, telling the secretary she had a weird question. The secretary immediately responded, "It's the time capsule, right? We get calls about it all the time." Unfortunately the time capsule was vandalized and no longer exists.

Recently, Allison's family decided to re-create that feeling of wonder by making their own treasure box, storing today's precious family memories in a unique way. Allison and Lloyd hope that with each passing year, the time capsule's sense of mystery and importance will increase for their children, now eight and four years old.

While professional time-capsule makers recommend using plastic or metal for longevity, the Strines opted for style over substance and fashioned theirs out of a sturdy paper-covered box. Olivia used rubber stamp alphabets to label a variety of small folders and envelopes, which were filled with thoughts, memories, dreams, hopes, and predictions.

"Children from toddlers to teenagers find this project enticing, while adults will reminisce about what a time capsule made during their childhood might contain."

ABOVE: *Like the capsule that contains them, the envelopes are tempting; interactive; and full of poignant, exuberant, and meaningful family history. When Olivia is twenty-three and Drew is nineteen and the lid comes off again, they will delight in recalling their creative and colorful childhood.*

MATERIALS

- photo box
- decorative papers
- envelopes, stickers, and embellishments
- rubber stamps (Technique Tuesday)
- découpage glue (Mod Podge)
- basic tool kit

1. Decorate envelopes using labels and rubber stamps to identify the contents.

2. Fill the envelopes with photos, notes, lists, artwork, and everyday ephemera.

3. Topics for the time capsule envelopes might include the following: Our House, Art, Today, School Papers, Dreams, Family, Hopes, We Predict, Coins, Favorite Magazines, Food, Games, Books, and Movies.

OPPOSITE: *A far cry from a cold, metal time capsule under six feet of dirt, the Strine family dressed their time capsule as if it was going to a party. Candy colors, a family photo, and exuberant ties make the outside package irresistible and invit-ing. It will surely test the resolve of the family not to peek inside for fifteen years.*

OTHER FUN IDEAS FOR CREATING TIME CAPSULES

- *ticket stubs, travel itineraries, and hotel stationery*
- *menus, wine labels, matchbook covers, and business cards*
- *favorite quotes, song lyrics, poems, and prayers*
- *children's drawings and other family artwork*
- *cards, letters, postcards, telegrams, stamps, envelopes, and printed email*
- *maps and house plans*
- *official documents such as birth certificates, report cards, passports, and awards*
- *photocopies of your hand or a group of hands, thumbprints, or hand prints*
- *political or current-events memorabilia such as newspaper clippings*
- *professional and candid portraits, vacation photos, photos of the inside and outside of your home and your family members' homes, reproductions of antique photos, and school or team photos*
- *jewelry and other small items or family heirlooms*
- *personal items that individuals might have carried with them such as a wallet, medallion, religious object, key or keychain, or lucky coin*
- *pressed flowers, leaves, feathers, and locks of hair*
- *small articles of clothing such as a scarf, tie, or handkerchief*
- *items that document an era such as a fax; a computer mouse; newspaper clippings; train schedule; advertisements for clothes, computers or cars; the cover of a contemporary magazine; and paper money or coins (which some experts feel will be obsolete in the future)*

Even the youngest children can participate in making a dream journal; simply have them draw a picture of the things they wish for and you can write down their words.

Wishes and Dreams

ARTIST: *Suzee Gallagher*

At times, our wishes and dreams might float to the surface abstractly, as in a summer reverie. Other times, they may be brought into focus through meticulous and introspective journaling.

At the Gallagher household, capturing dreams and wishes often happens when four-year-old Lucy sits at the kitchen counter, painting, experimenting, and making books with her mother, Suzee.

BELOW: *Along with delicious citrus colors, this book cover plays with type sizes and a clever juxtaposition of an ordinary manila envelope with flashy beads and a bracelet. Matte and shiny surfaces in the same colors add contrast to the lively layout. And who can resist the temptation to look inside every envelope!*

"If I can't find paper in the color I want, I paint it myself," says Suzee. "I create my own textured backgrounds and experiment with acrylics, watercolors, washes, and bleach. It is always the accidental discovery that results in something that is just right."

- manila envelopes and parchment paper in various sizes
- scrapbook paper and rub-ons (Jenevia & Co.)
- cut-out letters
- photo charm bracelet (Nunn Designs)
- acrylic paint
- foam brushes
- sandpaper
- epoxy stickers
- adhesive (ClicknStick clear mounting tabs)
- ribbon
- grommets
- metal corners
- basic tool kit

NOTE: For this dream book, include office supply stores on your list of places to find art materials.

Designing the Cover

1. Using foam brushes, apply paint to various sizes of manila envelopes and parchment paper.

2. Make copies of cropped photographs and gently rub them with sandpaper to soften the edges.

3. Affix cut-out letters and rub-on letters to the cover.

4. Layer envelopes, photos, and embellishments to create a balanced layout on the pages.

5. Make six evenly spaced holes at the end of each large envelope with a hole punch.

6. Insert grommets following the manufacturer's instructions.

Making the Binding

1. Cut a length of ribbon fives times the length of the spine.

2. Fold the ribbon in half. Starting at the bottom of the spine, lace the envelopes together.

3. Weave a beaded embellishment and bracelet into the ribbon on the spine.

ENVELOPING YOUR WISHES AND DREAMS

Suzee Gallagher's entire project is made from envelopes; large ones are used for the pages and small ones are attached to hold papers, trinkets, and journaling. Envelopes are easy to make in any shape or size and can be constructed from almost any type of paper. Consider old calendars, junk mail, catalogs, wallpaper, and scrapbook paper.

Envelopes are the perfect partner for journals and handmade books. From tiny glassine envelopes made for stamps to large manila ones from the office supply stores to the artful ones you create, envelopes can hold both your treasures and your treasured thoughts.

MAKING AN ENVELOPE TEMPLATE

To make an envelope template, carefully open the seams of a regular envelope, flatten, and trace around the edges. Cut out the envelope shape and use the original envelope as a guide to folding. Glue the edges at the overlaps.

MAKING A QUICK ENVELOPE BOOK

1. *Decide how many pages you want for the book. Each envelope will be folded in half, making two pages. If you want six pages, use three envelopes and an additional one for the cover. All envelopes should be the same size. Seal the flaps before starting. Fold each envelope in half vertically, with the sealed flaps on the inside.*

2. *Decorate the outside of one envelope for the cover.*

3. *Make a vertical fold in the center of the decorated envelope. Punch two holes on the left side (near the fold), one near the top, and one near the bottom.*

4. *Fold the remaining envelopes in the same manner.*

5. *Punch holes to match the holes on the decorated cover.*

6. *Stack the folded and punched envelopes and place them inside the cover, lining up the holes.*

7. *For the binding, use yarn, ribbon, or embroidery floss. Thread it through the holes and tie on the outside.*

8. *Decorate or collage the inside pages. Add sentiments if the book is being given as a card.*

Dreaming of a French Farmhouse

ARTIST: *Linda Blinn*

The setting for the story, *The Secrets of Pistoulet*, is a traditional French farmhouse converted into an inn. According to the story, magical mysteries and life-changing events happen to those who stay at Pistoulet.

With roots in the sunny hillsides of Provence, this farmhouse's design is rustic, warm, cozy, and appealing. The shape is a basic rectangle and the model is easy to construct from supplies found at general craft stores. Mediterranean colors come from the earth and sky:

warm golds, grass greens, brilliant cobalt blues, ochre, rose, and russet. The downstairs rooms open directly to the garden, and there is always a pergola across the front, planted with vines for shade.

BELOW: *This model house was inspired by the book,* The Secrets of Pistoulet.

"If you build it, they will come. Asking for construction advice is a sure way to lure the men and boys into your project."

MATERIALS

- miniature wood houses (here, three small ones are glued together)
- miniature wood buffets for doors and windows
- sandpaper
- miniature plastic roof tiles
- copper wire or twigs for the pergola
- wood glue
- solder
- acrylic paint
- blue paper
- clear acrylic glaze for the windows
- gesso
- basic tool kit

Making the House

1. Glue three miniature wood houses together aligning the sides. **NOTE:** You will likely need a second set of hands to assist you with this stage.

2. When the glue is dry, paint the house with ochre acrylic paint and "age" with a wash of burnt umber over the top.

3. Remove doors from the miniature furniture and paint them a contrasting color.

4. Glue the larger doors across the bottom of the house and the smaller ones on top for windows.

5. Glue rectangles of blue paper in the windows.

6. Apply two coats of clear acrylic glaze (Diamond Glaze) to the blue paper to create a reflective surface.

7. Glue the tiles to the roof, and whitewash with gesso.

8. Sand the tiles for a weathered effect and dry brush lightly in a few places with an accent color.

9. Fashion a pergola out of wire or twigs and attach to the front of the house.

RIGHT: *Experiment by combining miniature wood furniture with wooden models of houses, dollhouses, or even birdhouses. Doors from the miniature cabinets add architecture when used as doors and windows for the house. Hide your small handmade books behind the door openings.*

Making the Books

MATERIALS

- solid color cardstock (Prism)
- cotton fabric with a small scale design (Provencal prints)
- paper scraps for pages (advertisements, decorative papers, and torn pages from old books)
- embroidery thread
- needle
- basic tool kit

NOTE: If you want your books to fit into your dream house, plan the dimensions based on the size of the doors.

1. Cut a sample of the cover to make sure it fits into the opening. Pages should be 1/4" (6 mm) smaller than the cover on all sides.

2. For a 2 1/2" x 3" (6.4 x 7.6 cm) book, cut a 5"x 3" (12.7 cm x 7.6 cm) piece of cardstock.

3. Fold the cardstock in the center.

4. Cut a piece of fabric and stitch it to the cardstock on the front and back edges.

5. Cut four pages measuring 2" x 2 1/2" (5 x 6.2 cm).

6. Fold the pages in half.

7. Using a tapestry needle and embroidery thread, stitch the pages to the cover using a three-hole-pamphlet stitch technique (page 13).

MATERIALS

- manila cardstock
- colored cardstock
- ribbon
- paint chips
- fabric scraps
- paper scraps
- embellishments
- basic tool kit

NOTE: This basic accordion fold can be made in any size. The height will be determined by the size of the door opening. For this project, the accordion measures 3" x 24" (7.6 x 60.9 cm). Each folded panel measures approximately 3" (7.6 cm) square.

Storyboarding: Translating Wishes and Dreams into a Collage

Storyboards are used by designers, screen writers, architects, and engineers to bring their projects to life. For families, it is a form of creative play, usually with paper, scissors, tape, and glue. This activity gets your wishes and dreams out of your head and onto a place where you can see them.

The first step in making a storyboard is to collect clippings from magazines such as pictures, words, quotes, and drawings that depict your dreams and desires. No special talents are required—if you can use a pair of scissors, turn the pages in a magazine, and glue, you can do this.

If this is to be a family activity, gather around a table with some magazines in the center. Look for phrases and pictures that depict something you want to do as family. Also look for items you would like to have as a family. Don't limit yourself—anything goes—from an iPod to a home on a lake. Family members will learn about themselves and each other during this process.

When everyone has contributed to the stack, have each person talk about what they selected and why. Choose the top ten or fifteen images or phrases (depending on the size of the board you are using), and write a list of reasons each image or phrase was chosen. Arrange the images, phrases, and words on a piece of poster board or foam core and add more materials if needed. Adhere all materials to the board and attach an envelope to the back to hold the list that explains the images. Be sure to date the project.

For individual storyboards, consider specific categories such as travel, homes, activities, and things you want to learn to do—from painting to rock climbing. This same process can be done as a family book rather than on a board.

Designate a place to keep the storyboard and decide on a date when you will all gather to see if anything placed on the board has happened. At that time you can create a new storyboard or modify the existing one.

CHAPTER III

Here and Now:
Capturing the Present

IN THE COMPANY OF CHILDREN, WE ARE FORCED TO BE IN THE present. For them, now is the only time that exists. Artist and workshop instructor Traci Bautista has observed this joyful "in the moment" state of mind by observing hundreds of children in her art classes. "When children are engrossed in painting and making books, time does not exist for them," she says. Traci encourages this lighthearted approach in her adult classes as well. She appropriately named her bookmaking class Child's Play.

Artist Ruth Giauque believes that all learning should be approached as a way to have fun. She home schools her children and compares her daily life to a merry-go-round: happy, distracting, colorful, and somewhat circular. But there are those moments, she says, "...where everything seems to stop. These are the moments that cause us to sigh, gasp, and shout for joy." Ruth's journal, *Breathe*, recalls some of those moments as experienced by each family member.

Linda Blinn sees the kitchen as a place to mark the rituals of daily life. She feels family history is not meant to be summed up in broad generalities but rather in the smallest details—a sketch of the table where you ate as a child, an exquisite label from a bottle of olive oil, or a family recipe for perfect lemon bars. All these images shape and define our memories. She encourages everyone to keep a kitchen journal of these rituals and leave it open on the kitchen counter, accessible to work on "in the moment."

SEVEN WAYS TO LIVE THE MOMENT

- **CAPTURE** *the moment. Always keep a journal or sketchbook nearby.*

- **RECORD** *what you see and feel.*

- **LISTEN** *to the sounds and voices around you.*

- **WRITE** *down dialogue.*

- **KEEP** *lists of anything and everything.*

- **NOTE** *ten things happening right now.*

- **SPEND TIME** *with children.*

chasing waves... and being chased

drink a breath of sea air

Breathe, page 38

Breathe

ARTIST: *Ruth Giauque*

Through photographs and words, this family journal tells of the many ways we express emotion by how we breathe—be it a sigh, a gasp, or a whoop. *Breathe* marks those breathtaking moments in time where everything just seems to stop… and then you breathe again.

Ruth Giauque and her family layer elements together to link backgrounds and foregrounds. Each page combines simple techniques and uses transparencies, journaling, and the photographs they take of each other.

RIGHT: *Ruth added a flap, a metal knob, and some sassy beaded fringe to give this purchased spiral journal the look and feel of a portfolio. The style of the cover sets the tone for the rest of the book, with its emphasis on using words and fonts as major design elements.*

BELOW: *Although the faces of the three-year-old twins serve as the focal point, the use of words in many different forms give this spread balance and harmony. The varied text includes computer printing, rub-on letters, handwriting, and purchased fabric with printed words. The cover sets the tone for the inside pages, which are created with the same techniques and materials.*

- ✦ 7" (17.8 cm) spiral-bound journal (7gypsies)
- ✦ paper: Curry, Vida, Somme (7gypsies)
- ✦ two 1½" (3.8 cm) square pieces of glass
- ✦ gaffer tape (7gypsies)
- ✦ black ink
- ✦ book board (for flap)
- ✦ transparencies
- ✦ black acrylic paint
- ✦ awl
- ✦ sandpaper
- ✦ basic tool kit

Optional Embellishments

- ✦ assorted ribbons, including black grosgrain
- ✦ pompoms
- ✦ sequin trim
- ✦ black fiber
- ✦ beaded trim
- ✦ pressed flower
- ✦ clear buttons in various sizes
- ✦ "Open Door" knob
- ✦ rubbings: Mille, postmark, stitches, left bank (7gypsies)
- ✦ rubber alphabet stamps

Designing the Cover

NOTE: Adding a simple flap transforms a generic book into a portfolio.

1. Adhere patterned paper to the front of the book.

2. Use sandpaper to distress the edges where the paper and book board meet.

3. Using a utility knife, cut a square in the front cover the same size as your glass.

4. Sandwich a pressed flower between the two pieces of glass, and then secure them in the cover hole with gaffer tape.

5. Create a portfolio-style flap from book board and attach it to the back cover with gaffer tape.

6. Thread a ribbon handle through the holes in the spine of the flap.

7. Embellish with rubber stamps and trim.

"Art is part of the daily routine for the Giauque family—and when they lay down their paintbrushes, they pick up a camera."

Photography Tips

- Buy a good digital camera for the children to use. They can take unlimited pictures and any misfires can quickly be deleted.

- A photograph should say something about the person being photographed and have an emotional impact or a sense of humor.

- Older children might benefit from a simple how-to book or a class while younger children do better with only one requirement: the care and safe keeping of the camera.

- Be aware that the interesting and fun pictures they will take can be on par with the best photographic art.

BELOW: While her dad and brother run from the waves, Mikenna gets the action on film. Because children love to take photographs, the Giauques give their brood full photographic freedom with both disposable and digital cameras. These parents love to see the world from a 3 1/2' (1.1 m)-tall vantage point, showing all the interesting things that kids find to photograph

A Family Art Gallery...Displaying Art

Ruth's gallery at home starts with thrift store frames with the glass and matting removed.

Frames are hung in a wall collage or a gallery-style border. She tacks up finished paintings inside the frames and then rotates the artwork as children create new masterpieces.

- Framing your children's art and displaying it prominently sends a strong message to your child and is a wonderful way to decorate.

- Have your child paint a series of paintings on canvases and then hang the pictures as a group or individually. There is something amazing about painting on real canvas. Purchase inexpensive canvas in bulk; one is never enough.

RIGHT: This photograph meets Ruth's criteria for a good picture because it shows a range of emotion from amusement, anxiety, disgust, love, affection, and acceptance. We assume the dog is just plain happy.

GROWING ARTISTS

The Giauque children make journals and scrapbooks as well as paint, draw, and make pottery, jewelry and anything else they can dream up. Their parents' philosophy is to set them free to create in their own way.

Before embarking on something new, Ruth will often give her children a little technique instruction: uses for tools and products or helpful hints related to the project at hand. This information is not design related but rather the nuts and bolts of technique.

1. *First and foremost, hand over the paintbrush and step away from the project. The most important thing anyone can do to help their children develop their artistic expertise is to move aside and give them ample time, space, and opportunity to play, learn, and experiment.*

2. *You can still work with them and enjoy their creative process, but make sure it is their creative process.*

3. *Let their incredible intuition and artful eye guide them rather than imposing a "do it right" standard on their art.*

4. *Give them tools and supplies and even technique instruction to help make them comfortable and able to get started, but allow the magical creative process to evolve.*

5. *Provide children with their own set of supplies.*

6. *Pre-assemble a kit for each child with all the supplies for a particular project.*

7. *For a collaborative project, it can be fun to have children create individual pieces, then combine everything for the main project.*

Child's Play

ARTIST: *Traci Bautista*

Even two-year-old children will enjoy Traci's "paint with abandon" technique. The binding process is for older children and once they start, they won't want to stop. After teaching art and bookmaking to more than 1,000 children, she just might be onto something. Working with enthusiastic children helps to keep Traci's artistic spirit fresh and fanciful and she suggests that this childlike approach is one we all should consider.

Child's Play is especially well-matched for family projects because the step-by-step construction covers the skill spectrum from the simple task of folding paper to the more complicated one of binding. Everyone from toddlers to grandpa will be in line to paint the covers by moving paint around with a credit card. And because the pages can be made from everything from maps to paint chips, half the fun is gathering the supplies.

A Step-by-Step Approach

This project encourages experimentation and promises lasting memories. First, the children will be painting papers, and then, as they start to fold them into the book structure, they realize that they are building a book out of their paintings. Traci has observed that as soon as the children are shown how to bind the book, they get so excited to finish that they don't want to stop. "They will mix colors, tear papers, throw paint on the paper, and enjoy the process of creating. They never hesitate, they just go for it," Traci says.

A Teacher's Sage Advice

During classes, Traci keeps her rules at a minimum so the children will maintain a no-fear attitude toward creating art. Although she finds she must repeat the directions to keep them on track, most children are uninhibited. Make sure you teach children how to clean up after they make art. This is part of being a responsible artist.

- Give plenty of notice before you are going to end a project, so they can wrap up their final touches without being rushed.

- Break projects into smaller steps to make them easier to learn.

- Encourage exploration.

- Don't be judgmental—even if their choice of colors is not your favorite.

- Be supportive of their artistic interests.

ABOVE: *This book has five signatures, each with an individual cover. The signatures are first sewn individually with a seven-hole pamphlet stitch and then held together with colorful binding on the outside spine. Beads, bells, and baubles can be attached when finished.*

"If you need a [creativity] boost, take a break and do art with the kids; they will inspire you,"

LEFT: *Children swoosh, slather, and spread acrylic paints with a credit card in every direction during Traci Bautista's bookmaking class. When some of the paint actually makes it on to the covers, the result is a lively, playful dance of texture and color.*

BASIC BOOKBINDING TERMS

A folio is a sheet of paper folded in half. Folded pages that are nested together are called a section or a signature.

A signature is a set of printed sheets—folded to size—for binding together into a book. The name comes from old bookbinding, when printers left small marks, or signatures, in the margins to indicate how the pages should be ordered in the book.

MATERIALS

- acrylic paint (Golden)
- paint scrapers (old credit cards work well)
- 1" (2.5 cm) foam brush
- deeply etched rubber stamps
- foam alphabet stamps
- bubble wrap
- awl or thumbtack for kids
- tapestry needle
- waxed linen
- large binder clip
- beads
- metal cork-backed ruler
- craft hammer
- adhesive (CP the Ultimate)
- painting smock
- eyelet setter and punch (optional)
- basic tool kit

Making the Book

1. Create color-scraped signature covers by painting cardstock with two or three colors and pulling paint across the page with a paint scraper. Paint five to seven pieces of cardstock depending on the number of signatures you would like in your book.

   NOTE: Repeat at least one of the same colors on each signature cover to coordinate them.

2. Accent the top of the painted paper with prints from rubber stamps, or with textures from interesting surfaces such as bubble wrap. Dab paint onto the surface of a rubber stamp or a piece of bubble wrap with a foam brush, then press onto the paper to print the design or texture pattern.

3. Glue another piece of cardstock to the back of the painted covers to create a sturdier cover. Let dry.

4. Fold thirty to fifty pages in half (see facing page). These will become the book pages, or folios, of the signatures. Decide which pages you want in each signature and place them on top of each other. Signatures will have anywhere from seven to fifteen folded pages. Be aware that the more pages you add to a signature, the harder it will be to sew.

5. Fold the painted covers in half. Nest the folded pages inside the covers.

6. Punch seven evenly spaced holes in the spine of each signature with an awl.

7. For each signature, measure waxed linen three times the length of the spine and cut. Thread the needle with waxed linen.

8. Sew a straight running stitch starting from the inside bottom hole all the way to the top and then back down the signature until both strings are hanging from the bottom. Tie off each signature on the inside and outside bottom hole with a square knot. Trim the excess waxed linen or string beads for decoration.

Binding the Signatures Together

1. Place sewn signatures in order, from top to bottom. It may be necessary to hold the signatures together with a large binder clip.

2. To bind the signatures together, weave fiber, ribbon, or craft string in and out of each signature. Take the first string and tie it off to the top of the first signature and weave it through each of the signatures (under and over each sting of waxed linen).

3. Continue to add each fiber or ribbon by tying onto the waxed linen and continue to weave until you reach the bottom of all signatures.

4. Leave long tie-off strings and embellish with beads, charms, and tags.

LEFT: *This adult version of the book shows that anything you can fold is fodder for the pages. Mail art, envelopes, and ephemera make the pages interactive. Old book pages and maps can be partially painted over for a journaling surface.*

BELOW: *Multicolored raffia echoes the informal, lively theme of the books. Linen thread and fibers also make colorful bindings.*

MATERIALS TO USE FOR BOOK PAGES (OR *FOLIOS*)

- graph paper
- construction paper
- envelopes
- hand-painted paper
- handmade paper
- magazine pages
- dictionary pages
- old book pages
- file folders
- fabric
- brown bags
- receipts
- maps
- paint chips
- tags

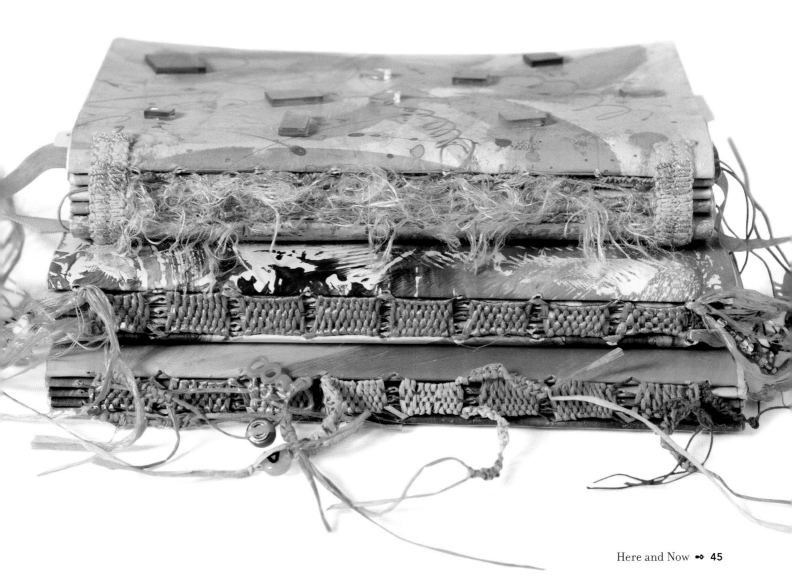

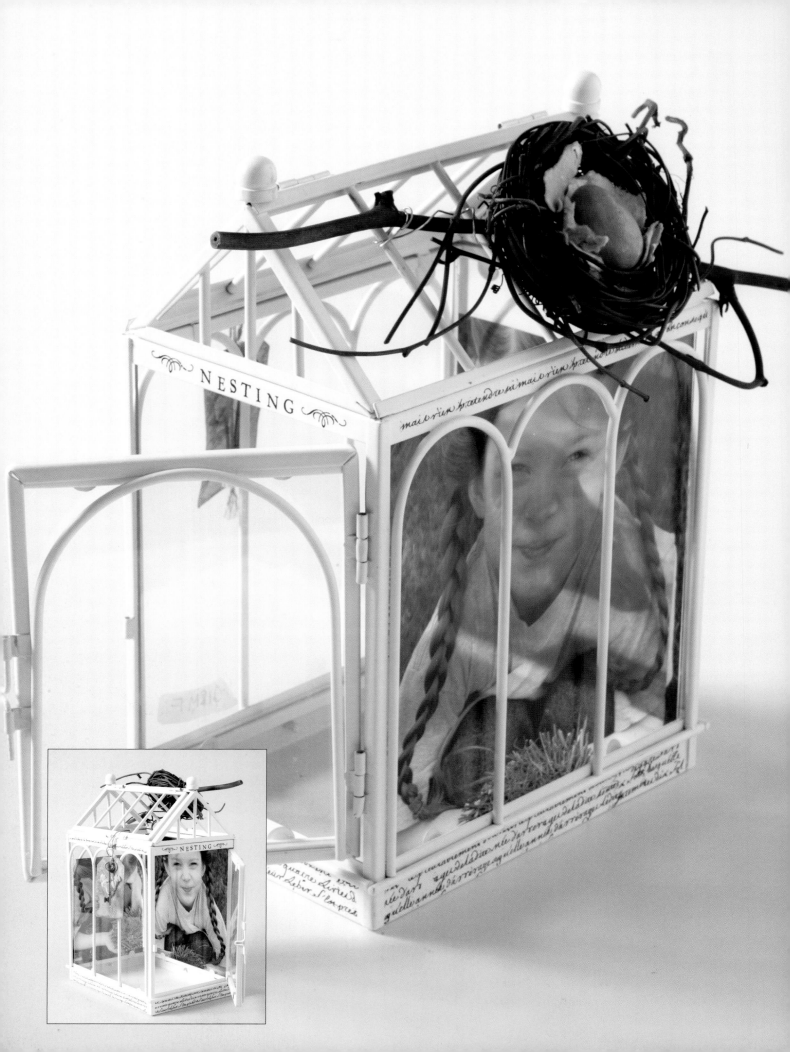

Nesting

ARTIST: *Ruth Giauque*

Using both symbolism and metaphor, this three-dimensional book project by Ruth Giauque and her daughters, Hana and Mikenna, is a combination of art, poetry, and papermaking.

Ruth's art reflects her trained eye for collecting objects. Her sources are junk stores, second-hand stores, antique stores, and her mom's garage. Favorite items include books, antique silverware, chairs, white ceramic pitchers, fabric, and ribbon.

When Ruth found a glass cage in the shape of a house at a close-out sale, she was immediately inspired to alter it and make it tell a story. Rather than placing the nest

inside the structure, the nest is wired on top of the cage, sending the message to these birdies to fly free as opposed to merely look out at the world through the glass enclosure.

As a child Ruth accompanied her mother to a poetry club. She may have been the only child in attendance but she listened and participated. Soon, she presented her own poetry in a local café and self published a small poetry book that she sold to her mother's friends.

OPPOSITE: *Airy and transparent, this glass house focuses on looking beyond its confines. Photographs of children are enlarged, copied on acetate transparencies, and placed inside the cage. The curvilinear natural forms on the branches contrast with both the color and geometry of the birdcage.*

BELOW: *Made from materials that any mother bird would choose to line her nest, this book cover is as soft and warm as a baby blanket. It appears to have been picked from a tree with its twiggy spine; after all, it is made from paper pulp. Poetry, papermaking, photography, and pencil drawings combine to make this a sweet project with a philosophical message.*

MATERIALS

- cotton pulp
- watercolor paper
- patterned paper (7gypsies)
- commercially made paper screen (or a piece of screen stretched over a frame)
- acetate transparency
- basic tool kit

Optional Embellishments

- walnut ink (7gypsies)
- tag (7gypsies)
- fabric and paper dye (7gypsies)
- key (7gypsies)
- rub-on text (7gypsies)
- wire
- birdcage
- wooden egg
- nest
- grapevine
- antique button

NOTE: Children are sure to enjoy the messy process of papermaking.

1. Tear up patterned paper and soak it in water. The longer the paper soaks, the less blending will be needed.

2. Pour the paper and water into a blender, add cotton pulp, and blend for approximately ninety seconds. (See the manufacturer's directions on the cotton pulp packaging for additional information.)

3. Empty the contents of the blender into a basin and mix in a small amount of blue fabric dye.

4. Transfer the pulp to a screen that has been stretched over a picture frame, or use a commercially made paper screen. Drain the paper-water mush.

5. Use a sponge or cloth to press the mush and remove excess water. Continue the process until all the pulp is pressed on to the screen. The paper will dry in the shape of the screen—usually a square or rectangle.

6. Allow to dry for several hours.

7. Mount the handmade paper on watercolor paper for stability.

OPPOSITE: *In just the right scale for the size of the book, the original pencil drawings complement the spare, keen poetry. The words seem to be airborne, ready to accompany the birds in flight. The watercolor paper background is aged with ink, and in keeping with the organic feel of the book, the pages are torn rather than cut.*

"I like trying new things and doing them in ways I didn't expect and having them turn out really pretty," says Mikenna Giauque.

For the book component of *Nesting*, Ruth was the author/poet, and Hana and Mikenna were the illustrators. The three of them enjoyed discussing the girls' favorite books and how authors and illustrators work together to create. Mikenna already has the right approach for experimenting with art: "I like trying new things and doing them in ways I didn't expect and having them turn out really pretty," she says. This is the poem Ruth wrote for *Nesting*.

NESTING

mother and father birds build nests
(they just do).
beautiful eggs
1-2-3-4
fill the nest to bursting
under watchful care
little birds hatch and grow.
they sit as open-mouthed stomachs
with bald bodies.
given time and space and freedom
they test tiny wings
and soon learn to soar
never to return to that same nest again.
i nest.
and you my little birdies
must learn to soar.
i will watch and enjoy and hope.
may the wings that set you free
bring you back again, and again and again.

mother and father birds build nests.

(they just do.)

i will watch.

and enjoy

and hope.

may the wings

that set you free

bring you back again.

again and again.

Kitchen Anthropology

ARTIST: *Linda Blinn*

From spontaneous moments to carefully planned rituals, the kitchen is the heart of family life. It may also be the home's most interactive area, abuzz with discussions, decisions, homework, artwork, and house work—all happening at once.

A kitchen journal must stay in the kitchen and, like a good kitchen floor, it needs to be spill proof and tough.

Granted, not all the artwork will happen on the kitchen counter, but the philosophy of a kitchen journal is more thirty-minute meal than gourmet dining. Pages are not meant to stay pristine—an accidental splash of tomato sauce may add some needed color. We are gathering and recording here, not producing fine art.

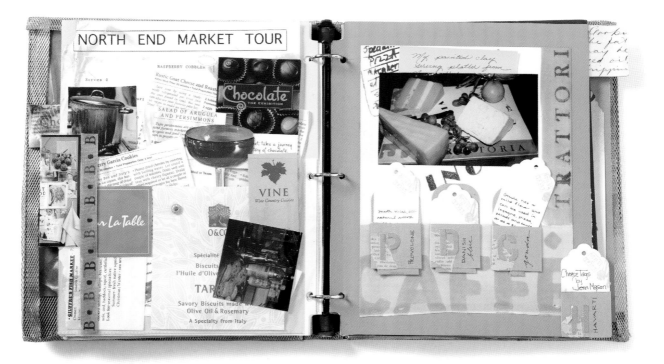

Start with a sturdy binder, generic pocket pages, and expandable file folders from an office supply store that can be modified and hole-punched to fit in the binder. Binders are convenient to work with because they open flat and you can remove and add pages at any time. Plastic sheets made for holding business cards and slides will also snap into the binder and hold the small items.

Materials Within Reach

One of the first places to find evidence of family life is under those kitschy refrigerator magnets holding everything from grocery and to-do lists to invitations, children's art, and photographs. Other materials for your journal might reference surfaces in your kitchen. Linda integrated copper mesh and copper paper in the book and photocopied samples of travertine from the floor and counter material to use as accents on the pages.

"Anyone who sets foot in your kitchen should be invited to add a comment or drawing to the kitchen journal."

OPPOSITE: *The cover of a kitchen journal opens up all kinds of possibilities to experiment with unusual materials. Think industrial strength rather than ribbon and handmade paper. Copper wire mesh, wood, and metal embellishments will withstand life in the kitchen. The wooden letters are covered in tissue paper painted with three coats of varnish.*

ABOVE: *On the left, a page protector cut in half horizontally collects business cards, recipes, photos, and clippings. These will be used later for pages in the book. On the right, a photocopy and photograph of a favorite serving platter creates a theme for the page. The photograph is also a pocket to hold journaling. Smaller pockets hold tags created to identify various cheeses on the platter.*

ABOVE: *Make background papers by dipping paper in a bath of strong coffee or tea, or by placing granules of instant coffee on paper and spraying it with warm water. Journal in the silhouette shapes left by the utensils. Photocopy silverware, table linens, placemats, napkins, and tile. Enlarge handwritten recipes on the copier to use as a background for photographs.*

ABOVE: *Because a kitchen journal is part recipe file, part scrapbook, and part family history, make use of your own items rather than purchased craft materials. Print recipes on transparencies to overlay on photos of food, and incorporate kitchen papers such as waxed, parchment, freezer, and doilies.*

Making the Cover

MATERIALS

- three-ring notebook
- wire mesh
- glue (E6000)
- wooden letters
- tissue
- old silverware
- ink pad (Metal Stamp Art)
- water-based varnish
- basic tool kit

1. Measure the wire mesh to cover the outside of the binder. Add 2" (5.1 cm) all around to fold over the edges. Affix with glue.

2. Adhere tissue paper to the wooden letters.

3. After the letters dry, apply three coats of clear varnish.

4. Affix letters to the cover with glue.

5. Add other embellishments, such as old silverware and stamps, to the cover as desired.

Planning the Pages

MATERIALS

- photographs
- recipes
- embellishments
- memorabilia
- pocket pages (from office supply stores)
- clear contact paper or page protectors
- expanding file folders
- handmade background papers
- plastic pockets made for slides
- heavy cardstock
- handwritten family recipes
- photographs of food and people cooking
- lists, labels, recipes, and menus
- old cookbooks
- food packaging: twist-ties, tags, papers, stickers, ribbon, and so on
- items representing your kitchen's decor, including paint chips, wallpaper, metals, and so on

1. Determine the categories for your journal.

2. Start collecting materials. Use the pockets and folders in the journal for storage.

3. Create pages using scrapbook techniques, your own style of collage, and journaling.

4. Assemble a kit to hold supplies and tools to work on your book. Keep it in the kitchen along with a camera to capture memories, mishaps, and mayhem.

Categories for a Kitchen Journal

Any experience with food, including cooking classes, dining out, and travel, are excellent topics for your kitchen journal. Shopping for food—at your local farmer's market, a holiday bazaar, or an open marketplace in a foreign country—are all part of the food experience. Other category ideas to fill your journal:

- holidays
- entertaining
- cooking with kids
- sketching and journaling
- favorite recipes

- written comments from family and guests
- menus
- wine
- food gifts
- food terms

The test for good food is that it disappears quickly. However, you can at least save the image, if not the taste, on film. And don't just honor your culinary masterpiece—photos of failures qualify for a kitchen journal as well. To support the theory that one picture is worth a thousand bites, some digital cameras now come with a "culinary" setting. Here are tips from the experts:

- *Turn off the flash and photograph the food in front of a window. The food will appear more fresh, natural, and realistic in the warm light.*

- *Consider cutting the food and zooming in for a tight shot of the texture.*

- *Food with geometric shapes photographs well.*

- *The plate or background should enhance the food (which will always be your focal point).*

- *Study the food you want to photograph, keeping in mind color and texture, and then look at it from different angles through the camera lens. Some food is attractive looking straight down on it, other items such as cakes should be shot "low" to emphasize the height.*

- *Take some shots of your plates, stemware, favorite coffee mugs, and kitchen utensils to keep on hand for pages in your kitchen journal.*

- *Photograph a table ready for guests or take a close-up shot of a place setting. Combine these photos with a copy of the menu for a journal page. Another photo of the guests during the meal completes the visual story.*

LEFT: *Some of the Blinn family's most memorable travel adventures involve learning about the local markets and food customs, and taking cooking classes. These food adventures are commemorated in their kitchen journal even though the kitchen they were cooking in was in another country.*

CHAPTER IV

Where Have You Been?

Traveling and Telling

WHEN THE SUBJECT OF TRAVEL JOURNALS COMES UP, I ALWAYS think of the Victorian Era, when an increasing number of ladies broke loose from the stifling conventions of their structured society and hightailed it to Europe and Asia, seeking freedom and adventure. While some filled their journals with botanical drawings, pressed flowers, and poetry, others wrote of riding horseback through Tibet and of rattling along in a horse-drawn cart through Finland.

Travel journals from the 1920s describe families piling into cars (rather than carts) with names such as the Hudson Super Six and the Cadillac Eight, then heading in style to Yellowstone National Park. These travelers took notes of their impressions; kept records of expenditures; and amassed collections of brochures, maps, and snapshots of places along the way.

Fast forward another eighty-five years and we are doing much the same in our mixed-media journals filled with "evidence" of the journeys we take. Now that we are able to jet off to exotic locales with grandma and grandkids in tow, traveling as a family, for some, seems to be the ultimate opportunity to create memories that can be shared by several generations.

Regardless of the era, anecdotes and narratives rather than facts are what make a travel journal come to life. Whether you are taking a relaxing cruise or trekking through a foreign country in search of ancestral information, journaling is not necessarily about complete sentences or perfect paragraphs.

Your powers of observation are heightened during travel, and with so many options and techniques for keeping a journal, other family members can find their own unique way to contribute to a project.

FIVE WAYS TO ILLUSTRATE YOUR PROJECTS

- **SKETCHING** *helps you to observe and be connected with your surroundings.*

- **COLLECTING** *ephemera and found objects adds interest and texture to your journal pages.*

- **PHOTOGRAPHY** *provides a lasting record and continuous supply of images to use.*

- **WRITING** *in a journal every day, even if it is just a list of what you did, all adds up to tell a story.*

- **COLLAGING** *the pages visually illustrates the places you go.*

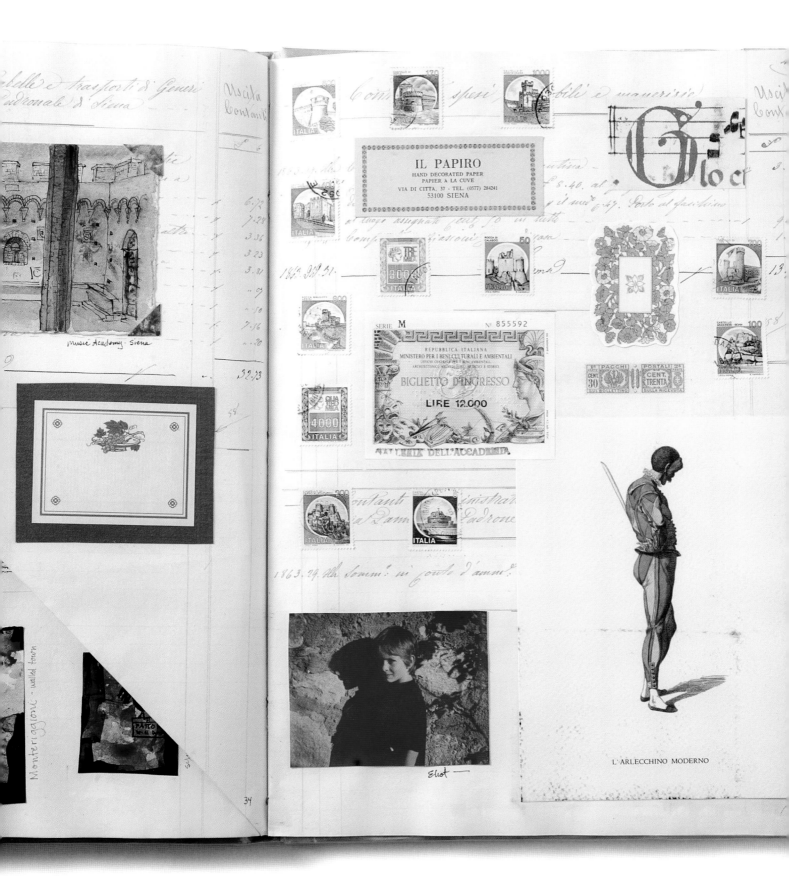

Music Academy - Siena

Monteriggioni - walled town

IL PAPIRO
HAND DECORATED PAPER
PAPIER À LA CUVE
VIA DI CITTA, 37 - TEL. (0577) 284241
53100 SIENA

SERIE M   N° 855592
REPUBBLICA ITALIANA
MINISTERO PER I BENI CULTURALI E AMBIENTALI
BIGLIETTO D'INGRESSO
LIRE 12.000
GALLERIA DELL'ACCADEMIA

Eliot

L'ARLECCHINO MODERNO

Italian Journal

ARTIST: *Jill Littlewood*

Traveling with a group of home-school families, artist and instructor Jill Littlewood unearthed an old farm ledger while sleuthing around a tourist shop in Italy. The old pages became the background for her various art forms and journaling during their stay at a Tuscan farm.

Waiting until you arrive at your destination to find the perfect journal may add another layer of intrigue to your stories. And, with a little traveler's luck, the journal may find you first.

BELOW: *If she had not glanced under the dusty copper pot sitting on the shelf of a store, Jill would have passed by the old ledger. But the parchment cover caught her eye, and being a papermaker, she could tell the pages inside were in perfect condition—150 years old and as clean and crisp as the day they were made. Each page had copperplate script written in brown ink all over it, with flourishes at the end of the page where the bookkeeper signed the page. She discovered the book kept the accounts of a large farm called a Fattitoria. The pages told how much olive oil, lentils, wheat grain, or produce a given tenant had produced and how much they had consumed.*

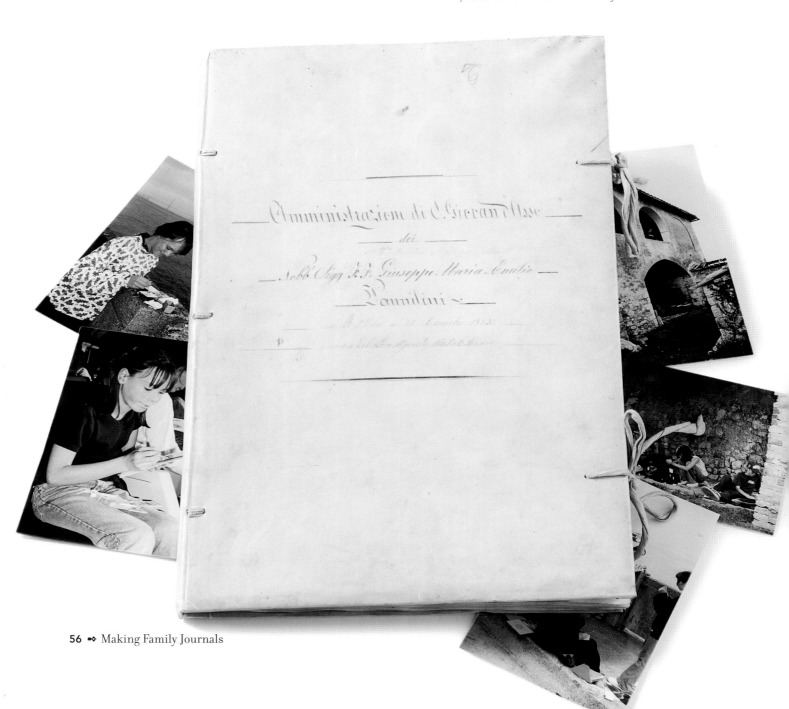

"As the days passed, beautiful books emerged. Some were done on papers, found or purchased, but each student also incorporated the handmade papers they had made in my studio back home. The books had the tender charms of young artists… jewels full of personal meaning."

MATERIALS

For making rubbings while traveling:

- handmade and decorative papers
- masking tape
- crayons
- charcoal sticks
- pastel sticks
- brushes
- scissors
- moistened towelettes

For collecting ephemera:

- envelopes of various sizes
- markers

- self-stick note pads
- tape
- glue sticks
- zip lock bags
- paper tubes

For painting and sketching:

- small watercolor kit
- water vial with cap
- spiral bound paper pads
- colored, charcoal and lead pencils
- masking tape

NOTE: Nicholson's Peerless Transparent Water Colors are self-blending water colors on film leaflets. The colors are a heavy film of highly concentrated pure color which release when it comes into contact with water. The entire book of colors will fit in a small space and is very light weight.

This adventure started as a "traveling art club" for six home schoolers, ages ten to thirteen. They met with Jill Littlewood in her kitchen, yard, and in various locations around Santa Barbara. Using travel-sized watercolor kits, she showed her students how to document what they were looking at and how to keep working when the sun disappeared, the wind came up, or someone wanted to talk to them while they were painting.

An Artful Destination

After two years of this Jill thought her artists needed to see some real art. What better place than Italy? She proposed to them, and their families, a month-long trip to paint, draw, study lettering, and immerse themselves in art. Twenty people went to the Villa Spannocchia, a magical place close to Siena. This lovely villa is the home of the Count Cellini, his daughter, and her family. They have been restoring the thirteenth- and sixteenth-century buildings and returning the land to its original functions: they farm organically, raise heirloom livestock, and work to restore the decaying architecture. Needless to say, the villa was as exciting and romantic as anything they could have dreamed up when planning this trip. Everyone spent time exploring the fields and forests and meeting the Count, his family, and other guests. They even got to help with the wine harvest and see the olives pressed.

Finding Places to Create

The first thing they did at the villa was to make one room a scriptorium—a room dedicated to writing and working in their journals. They traveled to towns in Tuscany every other day. In between, they worked in the sun-filled classroom where Jill guided the students through letterforms, serifs, gilding, book folds, watercolor techniques, architectural rendering, and the problems of working outdoors. Often the sketches that were started on the outings were finished in that room. As the days passed, beautiful books emerged. Some were done on found or purchased papers, but each student also incorporated the handmade papers they had made back home. The books had the tender charms of young artists: small pockets held ticket stubs, Astrix gum wrappers were meticulously glued down, and metallic candy papers were used as borders for drawings. There were secret messages Jill never read. There were tiny books bound within the main journal. These were jewels full of personal meaning.

Working in a Bound Book

Jill's journal was in process as well. The cover of the old farm ledger she found in Italy was parchment over boards and it was falling off because the leather cords that originally held the signatures together had disintegrated. She knew at some point she would need to take it apart and rebind the ledger. While traveling in Italy, Jill kept the book intact as best she could and glued drawings, rubbings, and collaged bits right onto the pages. It was only after she came home that she took the book apart, with some trepidation. Luckily, the binding was simple so she was able to sew her newly formed signatures onto linen tapes and weave these into the original holes the leather straps had gone through.

Jill also included rubbings in her journal. Italy is filled with carved inscriptions, and having brought papers and crayons for this purpose, she was delighted to collect an assortment of rubbings. They ranged from early Roman lettering found on the Coliseum in Rome to prisoners' scratchings at the prison in the Doge's palace in Venice to—her favorite—a gravestone rubbing of the wife of the count who owned the estate they stayed in. She was an American whose last name was Alden, the same name as Jill's middle name!

Her lovely students are college age now, but whenever they see each other they reminisce about this trip. Because of all their adventures, each has their own memories and beautiful journals as well.

MAKING PAPER RUBBINGS

Jill also layered rubbings made from architectural details, floors, and metal objects on to her journal pages. She used handmade and Japanese papers and metallic crayons to capture designs, textures, and words.

To reveal a motif, affix paper to the surface of the design with masking tape and rub the paper with the side of the crayon. It is a good idea to practice with your supplies before traveling and always note the date and place where you did the rubbing.

MANY WAYS TO TELL A STORY: DESIGN IDEAS FOR CREATING A TRAVEL JOURNAL

These families used every opportunity to tell their travel stories with words, imagery, and items found along the way. Their teacher's journaling techniques travel well, whether in a foreign country or in a neighboring town.

- Layer sheets of paper by adhering them at different levels on the page.
- Intersperse your photographs with purchased ones that show unique shots of the same area.

- Incorporate themes into your layouts such as faces, colors, local motifs, doorways and windows, and food and wine.
- Highlight favorite cities with a complete spread.
- Collect food labels for their colors, fonts, and graphic styles—see page 59.
- Tuck journaling notes into envelopes found along the way.

- Mix the mundane (tea bags) with the magnificent (gold-foiled coat of arms).
- Gather stamps, stickers, labels, and tickets together for a layout.
- Make compositions from small sketches and paintings.
- Use purchased wrapping paper as a background.
- Add a signature of decorative papers to a travel journal.

La Familia, *South of the Border*

ARTISTS: *The Adolph Family—Erik, Christine, Alexandra, and Lauren*

There are family vacations and then there are family vacations. During this spring getaway, twenty-five family members gathered together for a cruise. Christine and Erik Adolph and their daughters Alexandra and Lauren were enthusiastically on board for this nautical adventure. With a blank journal ready to be transformed, each played a part in documenting the daily shipboard activities: Alexandra and Christine did the journaling, Lauren found ephemera and made collages, Erik was the designated photographer, and along the way, aunts and cousins were welcomed to join in.

Christine's personal line of scrapbook paper is mixed with Mexican images and items found during their adventures. The result is a colorful and festive journal capturing the daily activities of three generations on the high seas and in exotic ports of call.

"Cruising is all about bingo and the food," laughs Christine. "After losing our floor space in the lounge to the bingo crowd, we ended up back in our cabins journaling on the beds." It wasn't until the last day of the trip that they finally found a perfect place to spread out their supplies: an empty conference room with a huge table.

"The journal was a bonus for the entire family, keeping the young cousins occupied while putting together a memento that will recall this lovely cruise for all of us," says Christine. "I just need to remember to bring twice as many glue sticks next time!"

ABOVE: *Shades of blue in the pool, ocean, sky, and even the carpeting, provide a cool color scheme for mothers and daughters to use in their collages. The journaling enthusiasts came to realize that a great deal of floor space was needed for this family activity.*

OPPOSITE: *With a spirited mix of color, text, and images, a generic purchased journal and generic tab dividers are transformed into a vivacious journal describing a cruise to Mexico.*

CASSIE
LAUREN
ALLie
DYLAN
ZaCH
anDRE

It was so much fun for the children to spend day in and day out with cousins!

Cassie got really into all the stickers and was fascinated with "Rub-ons." She did this page with all her cousins names on it.

ABOVE: *Demonstrating that you can make a journal any-where—including beds—the young cousins make use of alphabet stickers and candy wrappers to decorate their pages. The finished journal is full of resourceful examples of using what is at hand. These are the items you can't buy but that give journals a unique character.*

ABOVE: *Christine commemorates the daily bingo game by using the card as a pocket to hold tags made from cruise line ephemera. Colors on lottery tickets and clothing tags complement the scrapbook papers. Christine applies a coat of acrylic paint to the back side of luggage tags to create a surface for journaling. Tied up with a jaunty bow, the tags are transformed into a charming embellishment to tuck into journal pockets.*

OBJECTS TO GATHER ONBOARD

- luggage tags
- tickets and plastic room keys
- menus
- brochures
- printed paper bags
- candy wrappers with the ship's logo
- labels
- cruise itinerary
- lottery tickets
- bingo cards

Final Touches and Techniques to Add at Home

TRANSPARENCIES

ABOVE: *Shooting pictures of children can be a challenge but with digital cameras you can keep shooting until you get the right moment. Erik Adolph told the children to make a silly face and then a cute face to try and get them to relax and act more natural.*

LEFT: *Alexandra's daily journal served two purposes: it fulfilled her homework assignment and added her point of view for the family journal. Note her candid appraisal of Acapulco: "It was stinky and hot!"*

FOLD-OUT PAGES

REFLECTIONS ON OUR TRAVEL JOURNALS

from Christine

- As an artist, I had to let go of the idea that this journal was my "perfect masterpiece" and instead just enjoy the collaborative experience of working with children who spanned the ages of four to seven. This journal was much more about the experience and activity than the end product.

- If I was journaling by myself I would have the paints, mediums, and ephemera out and ready to use. With the challenge of working in public areas with children, it was easier to use a minimum of supplies: paper, glue, and stickers. (We made enough of a mess—and spectacle—with just paper.) I made sure to choose papers that gave the painterly quality I love in journals.

- Because there were so many kids, each one had a separate page to create. This enabled everyone to work at the same time and share supplies. Pages were organized and added to the journal as they were finished. Next time we do this, I will prepare the backgrounds for all the pages before we leave home.

from Erik

- On our trip to Mexico, we decided to document our daily adventures with photographs and a collection of mementos in a journal. In our free time, Christine worked on a journal with the kids and I took photos and created slideshows on the laptop.

- Going ashore provided plenty of opportunities to photograph unusual colors and textures. I brought the camera everywhere we went during our city tours because we never knew what would be coming up around each corner.

- It is easy to compose a slideshow with a fun song on your laptop. This is always a good way to show off your new images. You can make a pocket for the CD and add it to your journal.

LEFT: An interactive page combines children's art, photographs, ephemera, and journaling, all sewn up together. A casual zigzag machine stitch is one way to attach fold-out pages and pockets made from acetate transparencies. This stitch also makes a simple accent frame in a journal or scrapbook.

Journey Journals

ARTISTS: *Allison Strine, Elizabeth Beck, and Their Families*

Allison Strine and her artist friend Elizabeth Beck were off to a five-day art workshop, leaving a combination of five children and two husbands at home—a noteworthy event for sure. While sitting in the airport waiting for a flight, Elizabeth opened her bag and pulled out two blank journals, one for each of them. Their purpose: a place to record every single moment of their week together. Before they even boarded the plane, the journals were well on their way.

By the end of their art adventure, the journals absolutely exploded with fibers, beaded binding, trading cards, stickers, and unusual ephemera. They took polls, documented every meal, rated every class, and wrote down ideas—no moment was too lowly to put into the journal.

"Are journals just a girl thing? No. Boys just do it differently."

How lovely! I have had a grand journey with three lovely companions. We visited lovely folks. We did lovely things... but now i'm ready ↑

Drew's Journey Journal

J.J's Journey Journal

Sophie

ABOVE: *Spontaneous, candid, and colorful, this collection of family travel journals bursts with brochures, business cards, thoughts, and lists. A sprinkling of flotsam and jetsam finds its way on to some of the pages reminding us that "beauty is in the eye." Four-year-old Sophie Beck covered pages in letters, glue, and mounds of stuff—a mixed-media artist in the making!*

OPPOSITE: *A fabulous week of art camp is now fondly remembered through two exuberant journals. After a wire mesh class, Elizabeth covered her basic grocery store-bought notebook in brass mesh. A beading class inspired the beaded edges of some of the pages. Allison plastered her cover with art trades, strange stickers, and weird ephemera.*

Journaling Is Contagious

With minimal supplies and a little nudging, journaling can become a passion. And, although the five kids and two husbands didn't expect it, they soon became active participants in the "journey journal" frenzy.

Julia Beck was the first to become infatuated. She read every single page of her mother's journal. She asked questions. She laughed. She asked to see the art described in the journal. And, most importantly, she asked when she would get to make one!

For the Strines, a journey journal officially became a tradition on a family trip to Asheville, North Carolina. Daughter Olivia saw the entire trip through her new journal.

"She challenged herself to fill every page with drawings and lists and writing and it was all so darn happy!" says Allison. The lightbulb clicked in her head: a journey journal equals entertained child.

Later, mothers and daughters were off to Florida with four journals in hand. Over the course of a long weekend, each journal blossomed with collected odds and ends that recounted their daily activities. They wrote and drew and colored and collaged the entire weekend. If there was such a thing as competitive journaling, these little artists would be the champions.

The boys participated in their own unique ways. Although eight-year-old Drew Beck is motivated by things other than

ABOVE: *In the Beck household, journals are proudly displayed on a shelf in the kitchen. For their version of a journal shelf, Allison and Olivia Strine covered a wooden shelf with travel paper and stickers to hold their growing collection. The display adds a certain panache to their library.*

journals, he too kept a journey journal that is now a prized possession. Currently, four-year-old Ethan Strine's claim to fame is being an avid "taper-downer" of things. He also advises his mom on her journaling—while consuming vast quantities of tape.

Here, There, Everywhere

CHILDREN'S JOURNALS

- *Journals should be small enough to tuck in a purse or backpack to keep them readily available.*

- *Carry the basic journaling supplies in a sealable plastic bag.*

- *Encourage writing of any sort; don't worry about grammar, punctuation, or spelling in journals.*

- *Let younger children tape and glue items into your journal.*

- *Start with pictures. Young children can describe an event with their drawings.*

- *Write in your journal while your child does the same.*

- *Let your child choose the type of journal and markers he wants and whether or not to share what he writes in it.*

- *Don't criticize, edit, instruct, or imply that there is a right or wrong way to journal.*

- *Make available magazines, photographs, and catalogs for children to use in collage.*

- *Give them prompts on subjects to write about whether you are traveling or at home.*

- *Ask an open-ended question or suggest they make a list of specific things to include.*

THE STRINE'S LIST: WHEN AND WHERE TO JOURNAL

- *in the car*

- *on a boat*

- *in a plane*

- *on a monorail*

- *by a pool*

- *at the kitchen table as a group*

- *while waiting for family members to shower and dress*

- *during restless mornings before an amusement park trip*

- *waiting for a meal in a restaurant*

- *in place of a bedtime story*

- *as a quiet-time activity*

- *secretly under the covers after lights out*

THE BECK'S LIST: JOURNAL SUPPLIES

Take a separate bag for each journal and include:

- *the journals*

- *glue sticks*

- *scissors (but not on the airplane)*

- *colored markers*

- *pens*

- *crayons*

- *colored pencils*

- *tape*

- *art papers*

- *cardstock*

- *stickers*

- *items collected along the way*

CHAPTER V

It Seems Like Yesterday:
Gathering Family History

FOR MANY, THE TERM "TIME FLIES" BECOMES MORE THAN JUST words when we realize days melt into months and we find ourselves wondering where entire years have gone. These are the moments to reflect on the importance of preserving your family legacy.

This happened to Jennifer Francis Bitto while she was looking through a box of family memorabilia that had remained in storage for more than thirty years. She came across photographs that she had never seen and that prompted her to organize a family project honoring her mother.

Jenn Mason had a similar experience looking at her husband's family albums. The photographs revealed an unusual trait in three generations of her husband's family. This inspired her to pay tribute to their adventurous spirits in her theme book, *Wind*. It will be a gift to her father-in-law as well as a reminder to her children that they may carry these same traits.

Whether these projects are called family history art, ancestor art, memory art, or heritage art, they become treasured and meaningful keepsakes. Theme books, albums, and three-dimensional heritage projects may also reflect contemporary life. In Jenn Mason's ongoing project, *Home Is Where the Art Is*, she is establishing an artful record of every house her family lives in.

FIVE WAYS TO PROMOTE FAMILY UNITY

- **CONNECT** *with extended family members to share information.*

- **GATHER** *documents, photographs, and family memorabilia.*

- **ORGANIZE** *potluck parties and reunions.*

- **COMMEMORATE** *your heritage with art and family history books.*

- **CELEBRATE** *the traits, talents, and values of your relatives while they are still living. Each successive generation benefits.*

Family Album, page 98

Home Is Where the Art Is

ARTIST: *Jenn Mason*

Jenn and her husband Matt took a backward glance at the locations they have lived in ten years' time: the Midwest, the East Coast, the Rockies, and the South. This book chronicles their life by the houses they've made into homes.

In this project, like building or remodeling an actual house, much of the time will be spent in the planning and gathering of materials. As you choose photos of your homes, also include those that convey your life there. Blueprints and plot plans make excellent decorative paper.

"Milestones marked at our five homes have included marriage, dog adoptions (and burials), the birth of daughters Becca and Abby, first steps, first words, new friends, and endless home maintenance and remodeling."

LEFT: *The house shape pays homage to mixed-media artist Michelle Ward's architecturally inspired artwork. Jenn started with a simple house shape. The foam core front cover and the back cover, made from mat board, are both cut out to be a house shape with a chimney.*

DESIGN IDEAS FOR A HOUSE JOURNAL

- *Create a two-page spread for each home.*
- *Use a dollhouse window on the front of the book.*
- *Find a heavy cover material and substantial paper for pages.*
- *Add calligraphy and soul journaling with the emphasis on texture rather than readability.*
- *Include a journaling envelope for each home to hold notes written by family members.*

- *Select one page of each spread to be filled with blueprint papers, photos, ephemera, and embellishments.*
- *Use black and gold mailbox address stickers for each home address and cardboard stencils to number each home to provide flow and consistency to the book.*
- *Keep bulky items at least 2" (5.1 cm) from the spine side of each page.*
- *Reinforce vellum with aluminum ventilation tape or other strong paper where the holes will be drilled.*

- six-gauge copper grounding wire
- wooden dowel, 12" (30.5 cm) long, $1^1/2$" (3.8 cm) circumference
- round paintbrush, screwdriver, or other tool with a handle approximately $1/2$" (1.3 cm) in diameter
- basic tool kit

Making the Coil Binding

1. Drill a $1/2$" (1.3 cm) hole into the dowel, 1" (2.5 cm) from the end. Slip one end of the wire into this hole to stabilize and start to wrap the wire around the dowel.

2. Continue to wrap the wire around the dowel in a tight coil.

3. Remove the dowel and cut the excess wire that is not part of the coil. To open the tight coil evenly, slowly insert the $1/2$" (1.3 cm) diameter tool handle perpendicularly between the first two coil rows. Continue rotating the coil, using the handle to open each coil row and create even spacing.

Creating the Cover

The foam core front cover and the mat board back cover are both cut out to be a house shape with a chimney. Inside pages are $1/2$" (1.3 cm) shorter than the covers on the top, bottom, and unbound side. Draw your basic house shape on newspaper to create a template. The featured project measures $12^1/4$" (30.5 cm) from the top of the roof to the bottom of the house and the width is 10" (25 cm).

MATERIALS

- $1/2$" (2.5 cm) foam core (for front cover)
- mat board (for back cover)
- blueprint paper
- blueprint tissue paper (7gypsies)
- decorative paper
- vellum paper
- ribbon
- stickers
- game pieces
- photo of window box
- paper flowers
- pop dots
- hammer and wrench charms

- large rubber washer
- small metal hinge
- dollhouse window
- wooden dollhouse shingles
- aluminum ventilation tape (used for heating and cooling ductwork, found in hardware stores)
- dark brown brush marker
- vellum tape
- white absorbent ground (Golden)
- foldable ruler
- basic tool kit

1. Cut one house shape from the foam core for the front cover and another from the mat board for the back cover. Attach strips of aluminum tape to the edges of the foam core cover for stability. The tape should run along the edge, evenly overlapping the front and back of the foam core.

2. Cut out a hole to fit the front dollhouse window.

3. Apply the blueprint paper to the cover. To create the appearance of wood siding, layer 1/2" (1.3 cm) strips of overlapping vellum and affix with vellum tape.

4. Add blueprint tissue paper to the chimney.

5. Cover the inside of the cover with blueprint tissue and decorative paper, making sure to cover over the inside of the window opening.

6. Use dark brown marker to stain the shingles, the window, and the trim, then glue the window and trim into place. (**NOTE:** Bind the book next; then return here to complete steps 7 and 8.)

7. Layer two copies of the window box photo (the sample was printed on printable canvas) onto the cover using pop dots in between for dimension. Glue in paper flowers and charms, and add stickers or other embellishments.

8. On the inside of the cover, randomly paint on the absorbent ground and scratch in text with the back of a paintbrush handle.

Making the Interior Pages

Gather materials: photos, decorative papers, vellum, ephemera, embellishments, stickers, rub-ons, letter stencils, watercolors, acrylic inks, ink pads, ribbons, and twine.

To create your interior journal pages, adhere central photos and embellishments. Leave open space for journaling, the home address, and dates. Add ink or watercolor paints or adhere decorative papers with a glue stick. Mix random sizes, colors, and shapes of envelopes to hold journaling and ephemera. Paint, collage, stamp, or embellish the envelopes to match other elements on the spread.

Binding the Book

1. To make a template for the coil binding holes, mark the distance between each row of the coil on a sheet of paper.

2. Cut this template so that the marked holes are 1/2" (1.3 cm) away from the left-hand edge.

3. With the template, front cover, and back cover aligned and lightly clamped, slowly drill holes at each mark, using a 5/16" (8 mm) drill bit.

4. Remove the template and clamp the remaining pages and envelopes together with the template on top. Slowly drill holes through the pages.

5. Stack and align the covers and the interior pages and carefully twist the copper binding up through the holes.

6. Add ribbon to the outside of the binding and glue the shingles to the roof of the cover. Return to steps 7 and 8 in the previous section to complete the cover.

Patchwork Memories

ARTISTS: *The Francis Family*

With their long-standing tradition of crafting and making art together as a family, it was fitting that this creative family collaborate on an artful gift for their mom, Martha. Jennifer Francis Bitto took the role as coordinator and assigned each family member a section or two to complete for the skirt. She asked that each person create a patchwork piece that reflected their relationship with their mother. When completed, the project encompassed values of their family life: church, creativity, adventure, and Martha's love of quilting.

With so many participants, ranging from twelve to sixty years old and with various levels of expertise, Jennifer knew a pleasing result would depend on some level of coordination. "As long as you have a designated coordinator to work on final assembly, there isn't a need for working alongside other family members except that it might be more fun!" Jennifer says.

Instructions for the Coordinator

1. Place a piece of masking tape on each section of the dress form with the name of the person responsible for creating that section.

2. Visualize the form with something hanging in each section.

3. Determine where the mini booklets will fit best.

4. Draw and cut out templates for each section of the skirt.

5. Mail individual pattern pieces and supplies to each participant.

6. When all projects are returned, hang them in the designated wire section on the skirt form.

NOTE: Jennifer, the coordinator of this project, filled the leftover squares with her art and mini booklets and added the ribbon, a monogrammed tag, and a strawberry embellishment to complete the project.

OPPOSITE: *Three generations of Francis relatives collaborated to pay tribute to Martha Francis, the matriarch of the family. They started with a wire dress form with a removable skirt and transformed it into a structure filled with pages and mini books replicating a patchwork design. Like a quilt, this skirt is made up of many different blocks and styles but remains true to a defined palette.*

"This collaborative project works well for siblings who may live in different locations."

MATERIALS

- wire dress form with removable skirt (available from www.stampington.com)
- photographs
- family memorabilia
- red papers in various patterns and textures
- eyelets
- jump rings
- buttons
- embellishments
- ribbon
- printed red twill
- acetate transparency
- découpage (ModPodge)
- polymer clay
- basic tool kit

Instructions for Participants

1. Follow the supplied pattern template for the size and shape of your project contribution.

2. Create a collage, mini book, or embellished photograph.

3. Leave room at the top corners to accommodate the small holes needed for attaching the finished piece to the wire form.

4. Return your project to the coordinator.

Transfers on Paper, Muslin, and Balsa Wood

1. Print a photograph (color or black-and-white) on to a transparency using an inkjet printer. Use the mirror image setting if there is text in the photograph.

2. Allow the ink to dry for two hours.

3. Cut out the image to fit the size of the pattern.

4. Cut paper, muslin, or balsa wood to the same size.

5. Apply découpage to the receiving surface.

6. Immediately lay the transparency image, grainy side down, onto the receiving piece.

7. Rub the entire surface for about forty-five seconds with a burnishing tool or the back of a spoon.

8. Slowly peel the transparency away. The image will adhere to the receiving surface.

Transfers on Polymer Clay

1. Prepare polymer clay according to the manufacturer's instructions.

2. Roll out to a $1/4"$ (6 mm) thickness.

3. Use the same transfer technique as above.

4. Bake according to the manufacturer's instructions to set the clay.

RIGHT: *This photo transfer on balsa wood shows Martha and her husband Chuck ready for a sailing trip. A metal washer is added to resemble a ship's wheel; the term "first mate" denotes Martha's nautical role on the family sloop and is a romantic reference to her role as a wife and partner for life. "A Heart Full of Thanks" is a photograph transferred on to polymer clay showing Chuck Francis as a young man with his father.*

ABOVE: Jennifer filled the books with family photos recently recovered from a box that had been stored since 1978. The cover shot shows Martha and daughter Christie at the beach circa 1965. The last page combines an optic lens, the definition of mother, and the letter M for Mom and Martha.

LEFT: Je t'aime is the title of this mini book holding a very special French poem Martha's parents recited to her as a child. "Je t'aime; Je t'adore; Que veux tu, De plus encore." (General translation: I love you; I adore you; That I wish for you, and so much more.)

Wind

ARTIST: *Jenn Mason*

Jenn Mason married a man whose birthright came with a passion for harnessing wind currents as a means to sail, ski, and soar across the land, water, and sky. Her objective for this project was to capture this fascinating family trait in words and images. She chose a children's board book and fashioned see-through window pages to alternate with pocket pages to hold journaling inserts. Children's board books provide the perfect substrate for a project like this because the pages are sturdy enough to withstand all sorts of alterations. Her choice of warm metallic colors, silver tape, and clean layouts evoke an engineered, masculine theme.

"Mom does the cutting and book alterations on this project then invites her daughters to join in for the embellishing."

BELOW: *A treasured Mason family photo from the 1920s sets the theme for a book about three generations of men and their passion for flying. A transferred image of a vintage plane provides an ethereal background.*

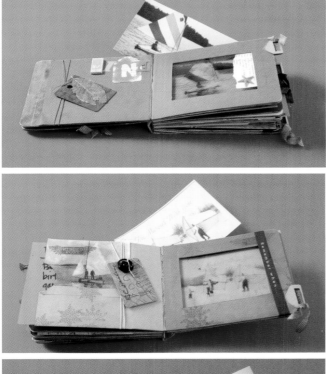

TOP: *Each carefully chosen element on this spread contributes to the topic. Orange linen thread echoes the rope triangle on the opposite page while diverse styles of letters appear to have blown in from every direction to spell "wind."*

MIDDLE: *In a 1940s-era photograph, wind-filled sails and ice skates propel the family across a frozen pond. This image was originally used as a family Christmas card, which Jenn made into a transparency. In flipping through the pages of the book, figures seem to be in constant movement, coming and going, as the background of subsequent pages come in and out of view.*

BOTTOM: *A hot air balloon, vintage airplane, and helicopter symbolize the many eras represented in the book. By using informal calligraphy the focus remains on the words rather than on the penmanship.*

Decorating the Cover

MATERIALS

- children's board book
- decorative paper
- ephemera
- tags
- rub-ons
- embellishments
- markers
- stamps
- ink
- circle punch
- blender pen
- basic tool kit

1. Cover the front cover with glue from a glue stick and adhere the decorative paper using a bone folder to smooth out air bubbles.

2. Use a craft knife to cut off the excess paper. Repeat step one on the back and inside covers.

3. To create the spine, stamp a piece of book cloth and then glue it to the spine using a bone folder to ensure good contact between the book and the book cloth. Trim the excess book cloth with a craft knife.

Cutting the Pages

1. On the first page after the cover, cut most of the page off leaving a 1" (2.5 cm) vertical strip. This will create the first short page.

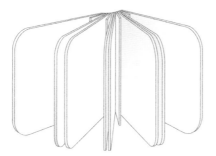

2. Skip two pages and repeat step one to create another short page. Continue this way throughout the book.

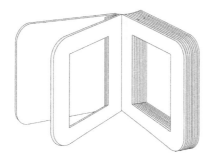

3. On each set of the two skipped pages, cut a rectangle out of the center of each page using a craft knife and a metal-edged ruler. Leave a border of about 1" (2.5 cm) all the way around. (This will create the openings in the window pages.)

4. Use a marker to color the edges of the entire book.

Making the Window Pages

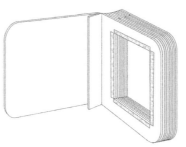

1. Small strips of paper are needed to create a finished edge around the window opening. Cut $^{1}/_{2}$" (1.3 cm) strips of decorative paper to the length of the inside edges of the window opening. Adhere these strips over each edge using a glue stick. Alternatively, a black or dark-colored marker could be used to finish the edges.

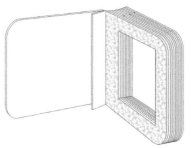

2. Using a glue stick and decorative paper, cover the front of the first window page in each pair and the back of the second window page in each pair. Use a craft knife to trim the paper from the window openings.

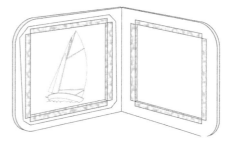

3. Set the first transparency in the opening of the first window page, using ample glue. Glue the first window page to the second window page creating the first completed transparent page. Repeat with the rest of the window page pairs.

Making Pocket Pages

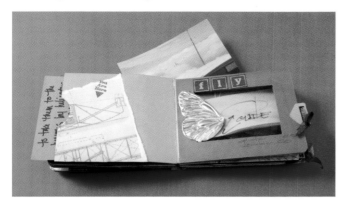

ABOVE: *Alternating with the window pages, pockets are added to provide a backdrop for the transparencies and to hold journaling inserts.*

1. For the pocket pages, cut strips of the decorative paper the length of the book page by two times the width plus 1" (2.5 cm). To make a pocket, wrap the strip around the ends of the short interpage, overlapping in the back and securing with glue.

2. Punch a half circle out of the end of the pocket to create a thumbhold.

3. Cut a strip of cardstock to fit in the pocket for journaling. Repeat the process on each short page.

Final Touches

Place laser copies of images facedown on the book and create a transfer by rubbing over the back of the print with the blender marker. Add stamped images as desired. Add other embellishments and ephemera as desired to carry out the theme and design.

CHAPTER VI

Long Ago and Far Away:

Ancestors and Genealogy

WHETHER YOUR INTEREST IN GENEALOGY IS A LIFELONG PASSION or a passing interest, technology has made research simple and affordable. From duplicating photographs to completing family tree charts, user-friendly software and thousands of websites on the topic enable you to step into the process at any level of depth.

Online genealogical message boards and personal family websites allow you to contact thousands of people with requests for information. It is even possible that much of what you want to know has already been documented and is at your fingertips.

Your approach to genealogy will likely reflect something about your personality and what is important to you. This chapter illustrates that style, slant, and attitude have a place alongside the facts, records, and documents usually associated with genealogical research.

The ancestor album compiled by Judy Rinks and Kelley Dunwoody accents the personal and artistic approach with mixed-media collages made from letters, recipes, heirlooms, and photographs.

The goal for Linda Blinn's genealogy project was to spark an interest by making it a family activity. The challenge at her one-day event was to find an area of interest for everyone, from grandpa to a lively eight-year-old.

Janice Lowry and Jon and Brent Gothold combined travel and journaling to commemorate their German and Irish heritage. Their books are full of facts, observations, sketches, and ephemera reflecting the countries their relatives lived in before coming to America. Personalize your approach to genealogy to reflect your passions, interests, and areas of expertise.

FIVE WAYS TO EXPLORE YOUR HERITAGE

➻ HISTORICAL *context will establish a timeline of events paralleling the eras of your relatives to help you understand some of the challenges and events that influenced and molded their lives.*

➻ ARTISTIC *transformation of family photographs and heirlooms will create more memories to share. Displaying family history makes a connection through time and helps children to build a sense of continuity and belonging.*

➻ TRAVEL *to areas where your relatives lived. Visit graveyards, heritage museums, and churches. Take historical tours.*

➻ PHOTOGRAPHY, *geography, and architecture tell the story of your ancestors with photographs, maps, and drawings of homes, buildings, and architectural details.*

➻ STORYTELLING *gives you the opportunity to perpetuate family lore as told by living relatives and create an audio component to go with historical records and pedigree charts.*

THIS IS THE STEEPLE OF THE
ALTSTÄDTER KIRCHE ST. MARTIN.
THE TRUE BIRTHPLACE OF THE
"GOTTHOLD" NAME. AS FAR AS WE
CAN TELL, THIS IS WHERE OUR
JEWISH ANCESTOR BÄR AMSCHEL WAS
BAPTISED INTO THE LUTHERAN FAITH
AND WAS RE-NAMED "CHRISTIAN GOTTHOLD"
ON APRIL 18, 1773 AT AGE 16.

JULY 24, 2005

AU OVER
PROJECT TO
DE FRANCE WHICH
EYRE. IT'S LIKE
THAT STARTED

THAT IS IN THE
CHURCH THAT WE
AMSCHEL AND
"CHRISTIAN GOTTHOLD"
KIRCHE ST. MARTIN,
BUILDINGS THAT WASN'T
BY THE ALLIES IN FEB. 1945

Good bless
you?
Austin Harper

A SITE OF A ROMAN
MARRIED PRAYED Baptized Here and
also payed debts Here

Spring

TRAUTZ

THE River ENZ flows
Right near this church.
During the BOMBING: [WWII]
People escaped to the River I₂
Because it was cooler. And
people from PFORZHEIM still
about the BOMBING Experience

A "modern" city
Becasuse of the
the WAR — THE BI
ARMSTRONG
town—
MEET BACK Here
at 11:30 am

Ancestor Quest in Europe, page 88
ARTISTS: *Brent Gothold (top), Jon Gothold (left), Janice Lowry (right)*

Picture Book

ARTIST: *Linda Blinn*

Some family photographs are just too beautiful to tuck away in an album or storage box. This one of our glamorous Aunt Apple is a conversation piece and a tribute to the legacy she left for future generations. Apple never spoke negatively of anyone, never complained, and always had a smile on her face and a joke to tell. She remembered everyone's birthday and anniversary and acknowledged them with a card and a phone call. Apple also loved to talk about the time she dated Clark Gable, and when she played poker in the 1930s with group of gold miners in Alaska. What a gal!

The first step is to find a used book or blank journal to fit into a standard, open-back frame. Measure the frame opening on the back. A book that measures ½" (1.3 cm) smaller than the back opening will fit in the front opening. We used a book measuring approximately 7½" x 9½" (19.1 x 24.1 cm) and a standard frame with an opening in the back measuring 8" x 10" (20.3 x 25.4 cm).

> "You will never lose sight of your ancestors if you turn them into art."

MATERIALS

- open-back picture frame
- used book or blank journal
- mat board
- printable canvas
- photograph (we used a head shot)
- gesso
- interference gold paint (Golden)
- basic tool kit

NOTE: Consider the era of the photograph when selecting a frame.

OPPOSITE: *Making art from family history brings the photographs out of the albums and up on the wall. This project, featuring a glamorous great aunt named Apple, is the first in a series of similar picture books for a family portrait gallery.*

Preparing the Frame

1. Cut the mat board to fit in the back opening of the frame.

2. Paint the frame with gesso and rub lightly with sandpaper.

3. Apply a coat of white acrylic paint mixed with an equal amount of water or glaze.

4. Dry brush interference gold paint on the frame.

Preparing the Photograph

1. Size the photograph on a copier or scanner to fit 8½" x 11" (21.6 x 27.9 cm).

2. Print the photograph onto canvas made for copy machines and printers (available at office supply stores).

3. Apply spray adhesive evenly on the back side of the canvas.

4. Adhere the canvas to the front cover of the book and tightly smooth it around the edges of the book.

5. Cover the inside of the book and the first few pages with decorative paper as desired.

6. Dry brush the cover with gesso and highlight with interference gold paint to blend with frame.

7. Fit the mat board to the back of the frame and secure it with nails or staples.

8. With the frame laying on the work surface face up, cover the edges of the front side of mat board with double-sided tape or mounting tape.

9. Center the book in the frame opening and press the back cover of the book firmly to the mat board to adhere.

10. The pages of the book or journal can be decorated either before or after it is installed in the frame.

11. To keep the cover of the book aligned with the pages, use hook and loop adhesive dots (such as Velcro) at the top and bottom of the inside cover and first page.

Ancestor Quest in Europe

ARTISTS: *Janice Lowry, Jon and Brent Gothold*

Meet Janice Lowry, a fine artist, her husband Jon Gothold, a graphic artist, and their son Brent, an art student. This is the story of their trip to Germany and Ireland and two very different approaches for finding information about their ancestors.

The German segment of the trip was a meticulously detailed itinerary for eleven Gothold relatives ranging in age from six to seventy. Leaving nothing to chance, Jon's parents, Jane and Stu Gothold, engaged the services of a travel agent, a German researcher, a tour leader, and a bus for everyone to travel in together. They also booked

hotel rooms in three cities and scheduled tours of specific museums, archives, libraries, and churches. Many of these destinations were located along the same routes their ancestors traveled.

Spinning off from the large group, Janice's goal for the sojourn to Ireland with her husband and son was to come back with a profound connection to her Irish heritage. Her strategy was the opposite of the Gothold's approach: She chose to simply show up with her grandmother's baptismal certificate and see what developed.

"An extraordinary adventure connects eleven relatives to each other and their past."

Different (Brush) Strokes

Whenever Jon, Janice, and Brent travel together they record their trips in visual journals. The pages reveal much about them as individuals through the unique ways they record what they see and feel. Brent's journal is completely visual and includes little journaling. Jon orchestrates pen-and-ink drawings, journaling, images, labels, and advertisements into well-organized layouts. Janice's style is to let her pages take her where *they* want to go with an eclectic mix of images— perhaps a watercolor painting, a prayer, and a menu.

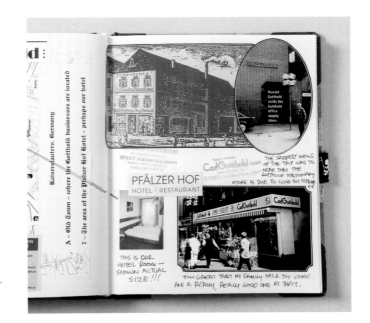

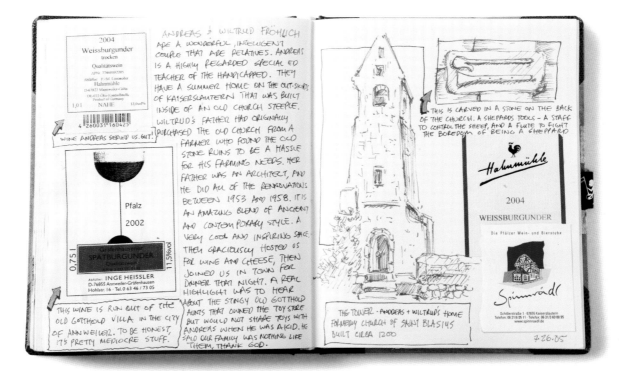

OPPOSITE: *Note the three versions of Altstader Kirche St. Martin, the birthplace of the Gotthold name. Jon painted it from the outside while Janice went inside to complete her depictions of the gothic architecture and the pastor. Brent captures a broader view of the area from his position across the river. He also collected a sample of water from the river (shown in his painting) to take back home.*

TOP: *One of Brent's defining moments of the trip was seeing his family name on a toy store because he and his dad share a passion for toys; Jon's toy collection is an ongoing adventure. Other family-owned businesses in Germany included a book bindery—a subtle enlightenment regarding Jon's obsession with vintage books!*

BOTTOM: *Jon was captivated by this 600-year-old structure located in the middle of farmland. Formerly the Church of Saint Blasius, it has been completely remodeled into a comfortable home, an example of blending ancient and contemporary style. It is owned by Jon's relatives Andreas and Wiltrud Frohuch.*

THINGS TO REMEMBER WHEN YOU GO OUT LOOKING FOR ANCESTORS

Jon Gothold

- Keep all your supplies in a small kit. Because you are doing "real time" journaling on planes, buses, and in hotels, you have to work in small areas with no room to spread out supplies. Windsor-Newton makes a nice watercolor kit designed for traveling. It can hold the paint and brushes and have room left over for scissors, craft knives, permanent pens, and adhesive.

- Be sure to take photographs of what you are drawing so that you will be able to compare your sketches to the actual image.

- Hang around in graveyards. Not only will you find the headstones of your dead kin, but chances are good you'll run into somebody living that knew your family. This happened to us both in Germany and Ireland.

- If your ancestors are from the Palatine area of Germany, chances are good that the historic buildings, churches, and records were destroyed by Allied bombing during World War II.

- If your family is from Ireland, nothing was ever bombed in World War I or II, so things from the 1800s seem like recent history.

- There is no one way to trace your roots in Germany. We hired the incredible Dr. Wolfgang Grams to help us find our family. In Ireland, we made no advance plans, showed up with a baptismal certificate at Janice's grandmother's birthplace, and found a bonanza of family history.

- The website www.nonstoptravel.com has a German roots page and many helpful links.

- Both the Germans and the Irish are lots of fun (and very forthcoming) when you hang out with them in a pub.

A SUMMARY OF IRELAND

Janice Lowry

- Ireland has many family resource sources.

- Take all known names and information about deceased relatives.

- Travel as light as possible; there are many stairs to those cute B&Bs.

- Stay physically active; travel is tough.

- Travel with an open spirit.

- Memorize the serenity prayer.

- Journaling and drawing are very creative and unique ways to document your trip. (Everyone takes photos.)

- Learn to draw and spell.

REFLECTIONS

Brent Gothold

By actually visiting where my ancestors lived in Germany and seeing the family toy store, I felt a connection to the Gotholds. In Ireland, watching my mother's free and easy approach, I also realized I have those characteristics as well. Travel gives me a better outlook on life. It reinforces that nothing is set in stone and reminds me that there is so much to see and learn.

LEFT: Here is Janice's journal spread showing the documents that led her to Clonminch Cemetary and the grave of her grandmother, Bernadette Parker. Maps, vintage photographs, and a newspaper clipping add to the documentation of this journey. Janice (opposite, page 91) is obviously delighted that she happened upon the Irish Heritage Center near Tullamore, Ireland. Many of these associa-tions, are located throughout the country and, along with along with the Irish History Foundation, and help travelers research their Irish heritage provide information about gravesites.

ABOVE: *Janice arrived in Ireland with only her grandmother's passport and baptismal certificate. She located her grandmother's gravesite through the local historical society and was able to make a rubbing of the Celtic images on the cross marking the spot.*

On to Ireland with Janice, Jon, and Brent

When Janice Lowry travels, her basic requirements are art supplies, journals, and time to draw. She had no preconceived agenda about her ancestral search in Ireland, preferring to leave everything to chance. Janice actually assumed that her red hair was enough to ensure that someone would walk up to her and say, "Oh my gosh! You are a Lowry!"

By chance, Jon, Janice, and Brent found the Offaly Historical and Archaeological Society upon arriving at Tullamore, the birthplace of her grandmother. This was a treasure trove of historical materials, family photographs, records, maps, and old newspapers. In addition, a full-time archivist and historian was available to compile a full family history for Janice.

One of the defining moments of the entire trip was when they found the grave of Janice's grandmother in the local cemetery. "We were expecting to look down and see a weed-infested slab of stone," says Brent. "Instead we looked up to see a ten-foot-high Celtic cross marking the graves. It was amazing."

And wouldn't you know they would meet an old friend of the family who just happened to be walking her dog in the cemetery while they were there. One would like to believe this person took one at Janice and said, "Oh my gosh! You are a Lowry!"

ABOVE: As part of their ancestor quest in Germany, three generations of the Gothold family gather in front of a toy store owned by their relatives in the town of Kaiserslauterr. Another family business, the Gotthold book bindery, can be seen in Jon's journal on page 89. (The second 't' in the family name was likely dropped when they immigrated to America.)

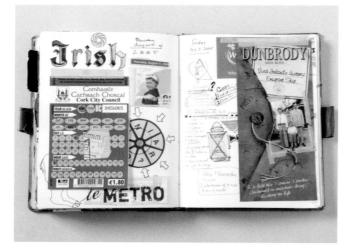

ABOVE: It is not surprising that Janice, Jon, and Brent would find themselves at home among the 200,000 book library at Trinity College. They are all avid book collectors.

ABOVE: Demonstrating their own version of plein air painting, the Gothold family enjoys comparing their varied artistic interpretations of the same landscape when traveling and journaling together. Janice always collects vials of water taken from rivers, lakes, and seas.On this trip, she returned from Ireland with a sample from the river near her grandmother's birthplace. You will see references to water in Janice's journal on page 93.

BELOW: The family set up their watercolor workshop right on the ground.

ABOVE: *Many images are organized in a nice composition on this spread. The shape of the steeple is echoed by the umbrella opposite, a small painting of a waterfall and container of water reference one another, and the red dots on the map are repeated in a larger scale to unify the page.*

Getting to Know You

ARTISTS: *The Blinn Family*

If her ancestors were calling to her through the years to learn more about them, Linda Blinn had effectively tuned them out. But when writing this book required a chapter on genealogy, she had no choice but to enlist her research-savvy children and grandchildren to grab their laptops and assemble some information.

Genealogy gurus advise you to first gather the resources at hand. For the Blinns, their best resource came in the form of Grandma Melba's pedigree charts. Her hand-written records, painstakingly researched—sans computer in the 1950s—furnished them with names, dates, places, and even photographs.

"Except for the cover, this project was completed in one day by three generations of a family."

BELOW: *The focal point of the cover is Melba May Trusty, shown as a link between the generations. Photos of ancestors from Melba's pedigree charts were resized and re-cut to use in various ways throughout the book. The grid layout is a simple way to visually organize many elements.*

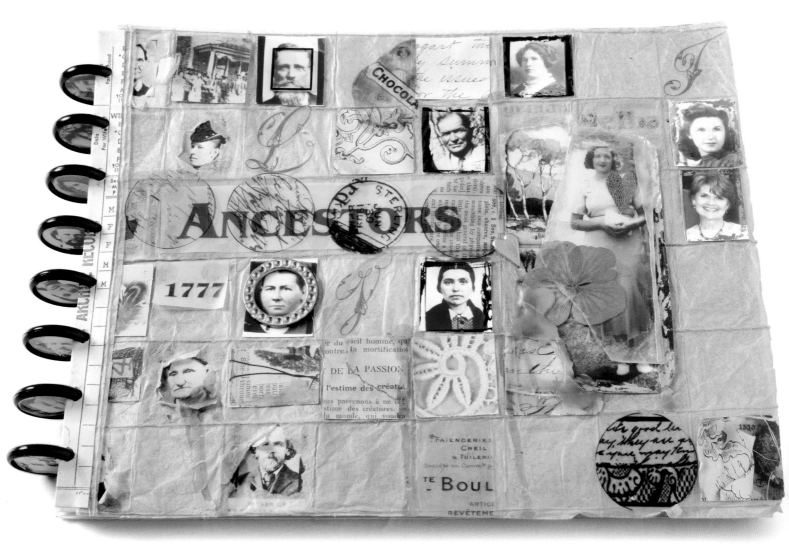

It became obvious that Linda's invitation to "get together and fill out pedigree charts" fell short of igniting a frenzy of activity to keep everyone engaged for the entire day. Pedigree charts are the foundation for tracing family history but after a while the factual aspects of genealogy—birth, marriage, and death certificates—lack the visual elements that make an ancestor book interesting.

The group took a different direction, exploring maps and websites to get a flavor of daily life in Massachusetts and of their relatives, the Varnums. Following a trail of links, they found that relative Thomas Varnum was fourteen when he and his sister Hannah witnessed the slaughter of three of their brothers by Native American Indians. This event happened about 1730 in Dracut, Massachusetts.

ABOVE: *Patrick, Tom, and Katie Blinn pick up the trail of research left by Grandma Melba more than fifty years ago. The Blinns photocopied letters, charts, and photographs from the book Melba had made and used them as the basis for an updated one. With the making of this book, five generations have now participated in documenting the family history.*

BELOW: *This spread represents the final phase of the Varnum and VanOrden's westward movement from Long Island, New York to Long Beach, California. The roomy Craftsman bungalow is a complete contrast from the previous generation's humble log cabin home in Idaho.*

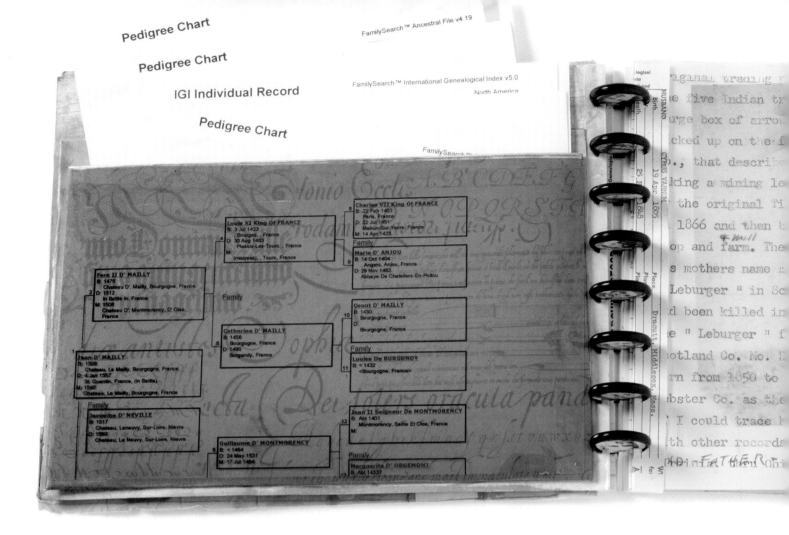

Making the Cover

MATERIALS

- decorative paper
- copies of photographs
- copies of writing samples, such as from diaries
- mica
- metal embellishments
- photographs of ancestors and their homes
- family photographs

- pedigree charts
- printable canvas
- acetate transparencies
- vellum
- maps
- round hole punch
- punch and binding discs (Roll-a-Bind)
- basic tool kit

NOTE: A landscape format was used for this book.

1. Arrange photos in a grid layout.

2. Affix transparencies, mica, and foil to highlight photographs with ephemera and embellishments.

3. Cut circles from the ancestor photos and adhere them to the discs for the spine (see "Creating the Binding," opposite page).

Creating the Pages

1. Copy and enlarge documents to use as background paper.

2. Enlarge old letters and photographs and print them on vellum or transparencies.

3. Enlarge a photo of a residence and copy it on printable canvas. Fray the edges by pulling threads loose from the edges of the canvas.

4. Print the pedigree charts in a landscape format. Note the day you did the research and sign them.

5. Make a pocket page to hold pedigree charts.

6. Re-size the maps to fit the pages and indicate where ancestors were born, lived, and died. This is a good project for children. They can find cities on a map, make small holes with a tapestry needle, and then connect the dots with a colored maker.

LEFT: When a photograph is overlaid with an old letter or documents, the reader is drawn into the story. Printing the information on transparencies makes it possible to layer more information on the page.

WEBSITES FOR BEGINNING GENEALOGISTS

Many of the following websites include sites for children to use and offer forms and printouts such as pedigree charts and family tree templates.

- *www.genealogy.com*
- *www.familysearch.org*
- *www.cyndislist.com*
- *www.familytree.com*
- *www.genealogy.about.com*
- *www.rootsweb.com*

Also try individual city and county websites, which can provide background information to supplement the pedigree charts. For instance, the Essex County (Massachusetts) website provides information on topics such as genealogy, cemeteries, historical sites, historical newspapers, and how to obtain records.

Creating the Binding

1. Make holes along the left edge of each page using a Roll-a-Bind punch. This system allows you to easily add and remove pages.

2. Use a round punch or template to cut photos of relatives into the shape of a circle.

3. Affix photograph to the inside of the disc. You will need eight discs.

4. Stack the inside pages between the outside covers.

5. Line up the left edges and insert the discs.

LEFT: *The round discs play off of the grid on the cover and provide another surface to embellish. Ancestors are lined up sequentially as in a visual timeline, one that also becomes a spine to hold the book together.*

Family Album

ARTISTS: *Judy Rinks and Kelley Dunwoody*

Judy Rinks and Kelley Dunwoody worked shoulder to shoulder for six weeks, but before embarking on a quest of research, design, and serendipitous discoveries, the mother and daughter team behind this project agreed on some very specific goals for their ancestor project.

Their top priorities were to do at least one collage for each person in the immediate family; share the treasured collections of photographs, research, and artwork with other family members; and create a lasting keepsake for Kelley's children and grandchildren.

After the priorities were defined, they could conceptualize the album and implement their many innovative ideas and clever design decisions. The result is a book that is much more than an album of photographs. Each detail supports the main concept of artfully personalizing, preserving, and honoring their unique family history.

"The decorative box on the front cover holds small replicas of the photo collages to give to relatives when they peruse the album."

OPPOSITE: *From its modest beginning as a series of baby photographs, this project expanded to a 10" (25.4 cm)-thick volume spanning nearly 150 years of family history. Personal memorabilia, poetry, art, ephemera, and photographs grace the thirty-six original collages made by this mother/daughter artistic team.*

BELOW: *Working side by side, Judy and Kelley often found themselves talking about the family's history, including memories associated with some of their recently deceased family members. In this photo they appear to have actually traveled back in time to meet their ancestors. They agree that sharing those sad and happy moments as they sorted through decades of memorabilia was the most significant aspect of their project.*

DESIGN ELEMENTS OF THE FAMILY ALBUM

Various-sized copies of the original collages are used in innovative ways.

- An onionskin copy of the collage protects the original under it.

- The decorative box on the front cover holds small replicas of the collages to give to relatives when they peruse the album.

- Miniature prints of the collages, printed on adhesive paper, are affixed to the back of each collage. These show the names and birth and death dates for each relative.

- All photographs were put on CDs for family members.

- The post-and-screw binding makes it possible to add more pages or remove exiting pages for copying.

- Copies of the collages can be used for cards and for other memory art projects.

LEFT: *Starting with Mary Porter Clymore, born in 1857, the book spans five generations of an American family. Judy Rinks dressed up her great grandmother with a bodice she fashioned from vellum, doilies, and buttons, accented with a lace collar. "Pearls of Wisdom" form a halo to complete the collaged portrait.*

ABOVE: *This collage of Judy's Aunt Estelle and her letter was a reminder of how fragile life is. Aunt Estelle wrote this letter shortly after Judy's mother died and only months before Estelle's own death. Judy keeps the letter as the focus of the composition, allowing Estelle's words to tell the story. Imagery from a poem in the book—stars, sky, shells, birds, flowers, and dewdrops—were chosen as cohesive design elements throughout the book.*

RIGHT: *"Grandad" (born in 1868) and "Daddy" (born in 1887) wear the same expression but very different clothing. The background pattern and colors give the composition a masculine, coarse texture. Another design element, the small replica of the collage on the back of each page, generates a flow to the book, almost if one ancestor is still joined to the others.*

MATERIALS

Cover
- cardboard
- decorative papers or onionskin paper
- adhesives
- grommets
- embellishments
- 2 posts, 2 screws, and 2 extenders
- 1" (2.5 cm) bookbinding tape

Pages
- heavy paper
- canvas
- photographs
- collage materials
- ephemera
- grommets

Spine
- cardstock
- canvas
- iron-on transfer fabric
- decorative paper
- grommets
- embellishments

Box on Cover
- small cardboard box
- acetate transparency
- embellishments
- basic tool kit

Making the Covers

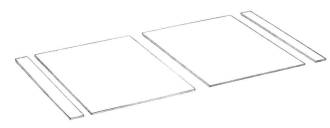

1. Cut two pieces of cardboard measuring 7 1/2" x 9 1/2" (19.1 x 24.1 cm) for the covers and two pieces of cardboard measuring 1" x 9 1/2" (2.5 x 24.1 cm).

2. Attach the 1" (2.5 cm) strip to the cover with the book tape. Leave a 1/4" (6 mm) space between the edges. Reinforce the back and the front of the 1" (2.5 cm) strip with a layer of tape.

3. Affix decorative paper to the cover. Set grommets in the 1" (2.5 cm) strip of the front and back covers.

Making the Spine

The spine comprises three layers. The side facing out is a piece of canvas decorated with a pattern from an image transfer. The middle layer is cardstock to provide support. The inner layer is decorative paper. (The transfer design used on the canvas is made from a photocopy of the decorative paper, so the outside and inside of the spine coordinate.)

1. Cut one piece of canvas measuring 7 1/2" x 10" (19.1 x 25.4 cm). Photocopy the pattern from the decorative paper (that will be used on the interior of the spine) to an iron-on transfer sheet. Apply the transfer to the canvas following the manufacturer's instructions. Add any embellishments to the outside of the canvas spine at this time.

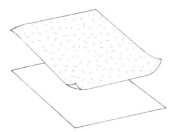

2. Cut the cardstock to measure 9 1/2" x 7 1/2" (24.1 x 19.1 cm). Glue the decorative paper to the cardstock.

3. Lay the canvas spine piece transfer-side down and then lay the paper side of the cardstock on top. Fold the extra 1/2" (1.3 cm) edge of the canvas around the cardstock and paper piece, and machine stitch a 1/4" (6 mm) hem on all sides. Insert grommets to line up with the front and back covers.

Making the Pages

1. Cut or tear pages to measure 5$\frac{1}{2}$" x 8$\frac{1}{2}$" (13.4 x 21.6 cm).

2. Cut page extensions from the canvas to measure 9$\frac{1}{2}$" x 2" (24.1 x 5.1 cm). Make one of these for each page.

3. Insert grommets into the page extensions to line up with the grommets on the covers.

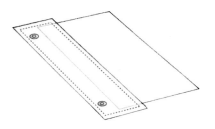

4. Layer one canvas page extension over a page as shown, stitch the page to the canvas, and then continue stitching all around all edges of canvas.

Creating the Box for the Cover

1. Cut out a window in the center of the box's lid.

2. Cover the box and lid with paper to match the album.

3. Photocopy a design on to the transparency.

4. Attach the transparency to the inside top of the lid.

5. Replace the lid on the box and glue a strip of paper down the left side to make the box open like a book

6. Embellish and affix to the top of the front cover of the album.

Finishing the Assembly

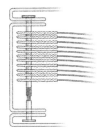

1. Assemble the pages in the order they will appear in the book.

2. Inserts posts into the back cover.

3. Thread pages onto the posts, last page first.

4. Use post extenders as needed.

5. Insert screws into the top cover and affix them to the posts.

ABOVE: *Kelley combined a romantic photo of her grandparents with a paragraph from a typed letter mentioning this "swell guy." She signed and dated each page and made a copy on onionskin paper as a divider and overlay sheet to protect the collage.*

ABOVE: *Each collage is copied on to a CD and card-sized replicas are made for sharing with members of the family. To hold the items, Judy and Kelley designed a decorative book-within-a-book for the outside cover and useful pockets on the inside.*

LEFT: *When Judy decided to use her father's handwritten recipe for pear relish as inspiration for a collage, the theme was easily developed by locating an appropriate photograph and a vintage print of a pear. Judy still makes the relish from time to time in memory of her father.*

Searching, Researching, and Recording

by Judy Rinks

GETTING ORGANIZED

- *Gather as many photographs as possible. You may be surprised at what might be hidden in family albums. Ask relatives to email photographs to reduce the cost of postage and the expense of making photos from negatives or originals. Be ready to share any photos that you have and be sure to say that you are planning on making a spectacular family keepsake.*

- *Identify each ancestor or relative. Writing the names on the back of the photographs helps to organize them properly for use in the album.*

- *When labeling your pictures, use the full name of the pictured relatives. This can become fun for other family members when they realize that they share a middle name with a distant relative.*

- *For newer photos that you would like change to sepia or black-and-white, adjust your photo in a program such as Photoshop. If you have a digital camera, check your owner's manual to see if you have a sepia or black-and-white setting.*

- *When scanning your photos for the CD, include other items you may have. For example, postcards that you have from a distant relative that mentions other relatives, as well as wedding announcements, birth certificates, military records, telegrams, greeting cards, and obituaries.*

- *Use an expandable file folder with dividers to keep the photos and memorabilia separate and accessible.*

MAKING AN ANCESTOR ALBUM

- *Experiment with printing on different kinds of paper. Instead of using regular photo paper, try acetate transparencies, onionskin paper, architect's drafting paper, high-gloss photo paper, matte, cardstock, sticky-backed paper, transfer paper, graph paper, or other vintage office paper.*

- *Make pockets in your album or on the individual collages to hold copies of important documents such as service records, birth certificates, wedding announcements, or obituaries.*

- *When documenting more than one branch of your family it is helpful to include a family tree. Numerous family-tree making programs are available at your local office supply store or online.*

- *Expand your collages by adding little stories about your relatives. This could be incorporated into the collage, added on the back of the collage, or tucked in an envelope.*

- *Another place for anecdotes is on the divider pages used to separate your collages.*

- *If you have family members in the military, incorporate one of their medals or ribbons (or a copy) into their personal collage.*

- *If you have old letters, cards, or postcards from your relatives, use these as backgrounds. You can also copy them and then use carbon paper to transfer their handwriting to your collages.*

- *If your relatives are still living in the family home, it is never too late to take pictures. Photographs can easily be transformed into backgrounds or paper to use in other parts of your album. For instance, the wallpaper used for the cover of our album was scanned from a piece found in a closet of the family home. Another idea is to draw a diagram or floor plan of the home while you are there.*

- *Find one photograph that you especially like and expand it into a series of collages. Vary the backgrounds, the colors, or the color of the photo itself.*

- *Polaroid photo transfers made from slides, scanned copies of photographs printed on photo paper, decal transfers, and transparencies give a unique aspect to the pages.*

- *Look everywhere for backgrounds and embellishments and try to find things for your album that are of the same era as the people in the photograph.*

WEBSITES FOR FAMILY HISTORY COLLAGE PROJECTS

- *The Library of Congress offers a printed ephemera collection encompassing key events and eras in American history. Whether you are making a time capsule, an ancestor book, or a collage, you can select from more than 10,000 images.* **www.memory.loc.gov**

- *Create a newspaper page of a specific era. Enter any date and get a synopsis of the headlines, a list of the top songs and book titles, and prices for everything from a loaf of bread to a house.* **www.dMarie.com/timecap**

- *The New York Public Library offers public use of its digital collection of images.* **www.digitalgallery.nypl.org**

Gallery of Shared Images

This collection of images comes from the artists who are featured in *Making Family Journals*. It contains original art, personal photographs, ephemera, French advertising art, and scans of fabric and three-dimensional objects.

Many of the images were selected to relate to categories in this book such as genealogy, kitchen journals, and memory art. Others are adaptable to a broad range of themes and projects.

Redefining Ephemera

The word *ephemera* usually refers to paper items. It is defined as "anything short-lived or transitory, lasting but one day." Mixed-media and paper artists have given ephemera, such as rare documents, vintage images, old letters, and advertisements, an extended life by incorporating them into collages, memory art, and handmade books. Photocopying and scanning ephemera enables the artist or genealogist to preserve the original piece, and allows the text and images to be resized, re-colored, and reused indefinitely.

This collection is for the personal interpretations and artistic techniques that will make it uniquely yours.

Clip Art Credits

JUDY RINKS: *broom, page 105; vintage clothing, pages 106 and 107; ocean photograph, page 108*

JILL LITTLEWOOD: *calling cards, page 109; calligraphy heart, page 113*

TRACI BAUTISTA: *art print, page 120*

SUZEE GALLAGHER: *round love tin, below*

All other images are from the author's personal collection.

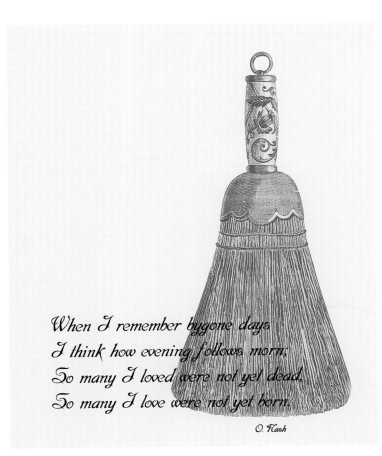

When I remember bygone days
I think how evening follows morn;
So many I loved were not yet dead,
So many I love were not yet born.

O. Nash

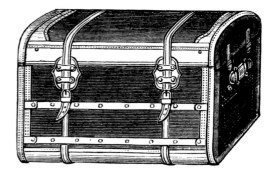

HONE'S
WORKS

IV

YEAR BOOK

BULLETIN
DES LOIS

7. SÉRIE
II. SEMESTRE
1824

General Rules for Meat

Meats must be weighed,
trimmed & wiped with
a damp cloth. It
should be removed
from paper in which
it has been wrapped
& kept in cool place.

Only tender cuts
should be broiled or
roasted.

When meat is to be
cooked by any of these
methods it is first
seared then the tempt.
slightly lowered. By
searing the albumen
of the outside the meat
is hardened & meat
is cooked in its own
juices.

For roast of beef
weighing less than
8 lbs. allow 10 min.
to lb. & 12 min. extra

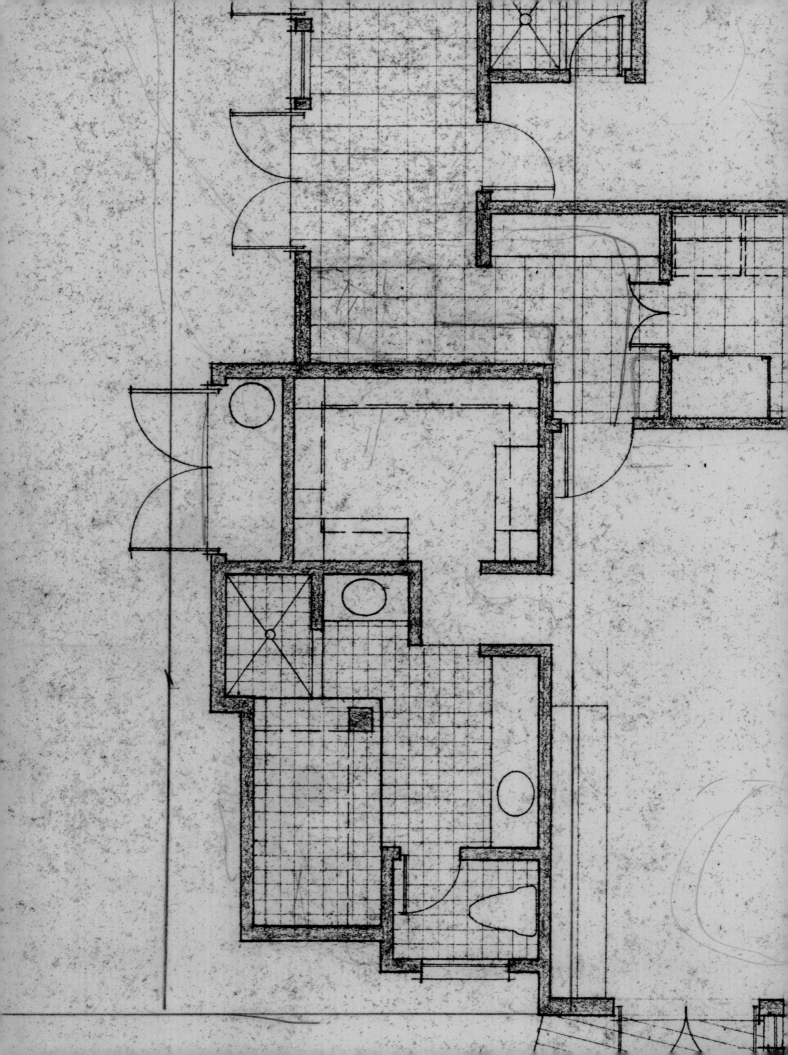

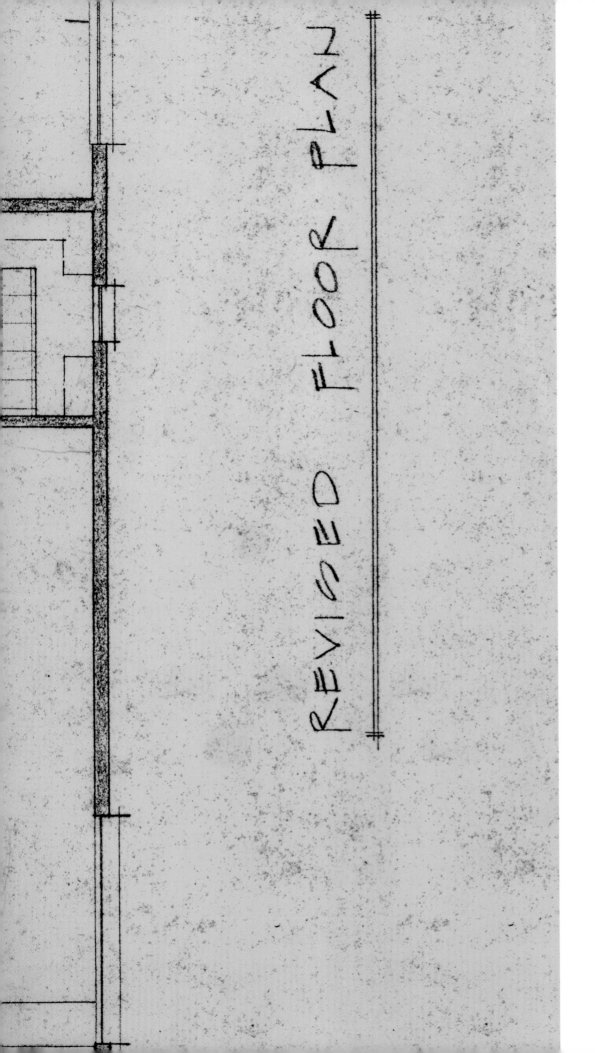

REVISED FLOOR PLAN

Exit writ to Sheriff.

June 8, 1936. at 2.10 P. M. served the within Sci. Fa. Sur. Municipal Lien upon Wm. H. Sponhouse, real owner and defendant within named, by handing a true and attested copy thereof to an adult member of his family (his daughter) at his Grove Street, Williamsport, Pa. and by making the contents thereof personally,

So Answers

o Paid Aug, 15-1936. Joseph Mertz. Sheriff.

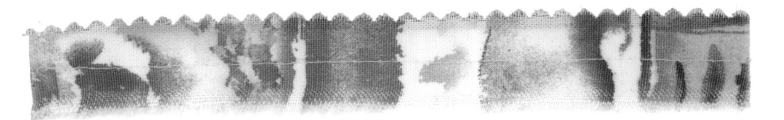

B. n.° 661.　　　　(173)

(N.° 16,672.) ORDONNANCE DU ROI qui autorise l'acceptation du Legs fait à la fabrique de l'église de *Gondrexange*, département de la Meurthe, par le S.r *Saunier*, de ce qui lui appartient dans cinq pièces [de] terre, [pour un]e portion évaluée à un revenu de 18 francs 5[0 cen]times. (Paris, 18 Février 1824.)

(N.° 16,67[3.] [O]RDO[NNANCE] DU [ROI] qui autorise l'acceptation d'un pr[é] [légué] [par] la D.e *Lelan*, veuve *Mo[...]* à la [fabrique] de [...], département du M[...]nan [...])

(N.° 16,6[74.] [ROI] qui [autorise] l'acceptation d'un [...] francs, [lé]guée par le S.r N[...] [à l'église de] *Bulle*, [dé]partement [de] Dou[...]

(N.° 16,6[7]5.) [ORDONNANCE DU] ROI [qui] [aut]orise l'acceptation d'une [som]me de [...]te en [...]ation par la D.lle *Lesage* à la [fabrique] [de l'église de] Plé[...] département des Côtes-du-Nord. [Pa]ris, [...] [Janv]ier 1[8...]

(N.° 16,676.) O[RDO]NN[ANCE D]U ROI qui autorise l'acceptation d'une maison avec [j]ardin et [d]épendances, et de dix-neuf pièces de terre, le tout évalué à un revenu de 180 francs, et offert en donation, sous la réserve de l'usufruit, par le S.r *Heim* à la fabrique de l'église de *Lhor*, département de la Meurthe. (*Paris, 18 Février 1824.*)

———————

(N.° 16,677.) ORDONNANCE DU ROI qui autorise l'acceptation de deux tenues convenancières évaluées à u[n] [reven]u de [...]

Contributing Artists

CHRISTINE ADOLPH

Christine Adolph has a BFA from the Otis College of Art and Design and a MFA from the Rhode Island School of Design. She uses combinations of mixed-media floral collage, surface pattern design and illustration, foil imaging, collage, paint, and drawing with acrylics and watercolors in most of her design work. She licenses her artwork for the gift, home decor, and craft market. She has designed three lines of stamps for Stampington & Co. and her products, Christine Adolph Designs by Creative Imaginations, include numerous collections of scrapbook paper and embellishments. Her work has appeared in many national publications, including *Legacy, Somerset Studio*, and *Cloth, Paper, Scissors*. Books featuring her work include *Pockets, Pullouts, and Hiding Places* by Jenn Mason, and *Beyond Scrapbooks* by Barbara Bourassa. Christine lives in San Clemente, California, with her husband and two daughters.

info@christineadolph.com

TRACI BAUTISTA

Traci Bautista combines her passions for making clothes, doodling, lettering, and doing "artsy" things into vibrantly colored handmade journals and paintings that are layered with rich textures of stained papers, painted sewn fabric, "girlie glam" ink drawings, and freestyle lettering. After a career in high-tech marketing, she is now pursuing her life-long dream of being a creative director and owner of treiC Designs. She designs [kÿL LäJ] girlie glam, an eclectic line of hand-painted papers, custom invitations, and aRt! kits for bookmaking and stamping. She teaches at art retreats throughout the country and offers private workshops at her aRt! loft in Fremont, California. Her artwork has been featured in *Somerset Studio, Cloth.Paper.Scissors*, and various books. Her first book, *Collage Unleashed*, will be available in July 2006.

www.treicdesigns.com

ELIZABETH BECK

Elizabeth Beck studied art history at Emory University and drawing and painting at Georgia State University. She has taught art to children ages three to ten. Her artistic interests swing wildly, but she currently most enjoys pottery and collage. Elizabeth lives in Atlanta, Georgia, with her husband and three children.

eandabeck@aol.com

JENNIFER FRANCIS BITTO

In the business of mixed-media, Jennifer Francis Bitto is a teacher, artist, writer, and photo stylist. She was the editor and art director of *The Stampers' Sampler, Inspirations,* and *Take Ten,* and was featured in *Legacy, Somerset Studio,* and *Art Doll Quarterly* as well as in the book *Pockets, Pullouts, and Hiding Places* by Jenn Mason. Her first book will be published by Rockport Publishers in 2006. Jennifer lives in San Diego, California with her husband, Ernie.

KELLEY DUNWOODY

Kelley Dunwoody has recently become interested in pursuing her love of art through online art such as Belle Papier. Besides collaborations with fellow artists, Kelley enjoys spending time developing art projects and traveling with her mother. Travel plans include a five-week sojourn in Paris with her mother and daughter. She lives in Jacksonville, Florida, with her husband, David, who is in the Navy, and her two children.

paris123@worldnet.att.net

SUZEE GALLAGHER

Suzee Gallagher is the consulting scrapbook editor for *Legacy* magazine and is active in many aspects of the scrapbook industry. She is a product designer and has her own line of scrapbook papers and embellishments. Suzee is known for her innovative techniques and advocates experimenting with use of materials—any materials! She is an accomplished photographer with work published in many national magazines and the book *Handcrafted Wedding*. Suzee lives in Villa Park, California, with her husband and two children.

suzee_gallagher@yahoo.com

JON GOTHOLD

Jon Gothold is a partner and executive creative director at DGWB, an innovative advertising firm in southern California. He has been in the advertising business for twenty-two years and has received many of the industry's most prestigious awards. His passions are antique books and vintage toys. John and his wife Janice Lowry live in Orange County, California.

jongothold@artype.com

RUTH GIAUQUE

Ruthe Giauque is one of the band of 7gypsies and her work has appeared in *Designing with Fabric* as well as *7gypsies in Paris* and many national scrapbook publications. She teaches workshops and hosts a never-ending art workshop at home with her four children. Her passions include photography, paper art, and poetry. Ruth lives in Gilbert, Arizona, with her husband and children.

ruthiepie7@cox.net

JANICE LOWRY

Janice Lowry is a fine art artist and illustrator and former instructor at the Art Center College of Design in Los Angeles, California. She transforms objects from everyday life into assemblages; makes her own journals (she writes every day); and works from her large, vibrant studio in the Santa Ana arts district.

www.janicelowry.com

JILL LITTLEWOOD

Jill Littlewood's work includes papermaking, letterpress printing, western and eastern calligraphy, traditional and experimental bindings, collage, printmaking, illustration, and painting in both oil and water media. Her work has been published by scientific publishers (*National Geographic, Journal of Vertebrate Paleontology*), commercial book houses (Del Ray, Crown), magazines (*Somerset Studio, Terra*) and private presses on the East and West Coasts. Her current project is all handmade paper and the "book" will be 80' long by 10' high (24.4 x 3 m) when complete—big enough to walk through.

Jill@Littlewoodstudios.com

JENN MASON

An accomplished and published paper and mixed-media artist by day, Jenn Mason is a writer and author by night. Mixing the two is her favorite blend. She started her creative career with a BFA from the University of Michigan School of Art and Design. As codesigner for Anna Griffin, Inc., Jen created artwork for national ads, television, and books. Her first book, *Pockets, Pullouts, and Hiding Places* shows her diversity in book making, altered art, collage, and memory art. *Paper Studio Baby* and *Paper Studio Gifts* will be available from Quarry Books in Fall 2006. Jenn lives in Keller, Texas, with her husband and two daughters.

jenn@jennmason.com

JUDY RINKS

Judy Rinks taught elementary art education for several years before becoming a high school principal in southwest Florida. Recently retired, she currently lives down the street from her daughter in Jacksonville, Florida. Now, with time to pursue her love of art and travel, she intends to fill her time exploring various mediums and concentrating on her first love, graphite drawing.

j.rinks@att.net

ALLISON STRINE

Allison Strine is a mixed-media artist who loves to play with paper, paints, fabrics, and polymer clay. Her work has appeared in *Somerset Studio; Legacy; Cloth, Paper, Scissors;* and in many national scrapbook magazines. Allison's projects are featured in the books *Your Sentiments Exactly* and *Pockets, Pullouts, and Hiding Places*. She lives in Atlanta, Georgia, with her left-brained husband and two children.

allisonstrine@mac.com

Resources

3M
www.3M.com
Transparencies, laminating supplies, and adhesives including glue sticks, specialty tapes, foam-tape squares, and spray adhesives

7 Gypsies
www.7gypsies.com
Scrapbooking supplies including unusual embellishments

Adhesive Technologies, Inc.
www.adhesivetechnologies.com.co.nz
Epoxy resins, adhesives

Anna Griffin, Inc.
www.annagriffin.com
Decorative paper and embellishments

Apollo Transparency Film
www.apolloavproducts.com
Acetate transparencies

Autumn Leaves
www.autumnleaves.com
Scrapbooking paper, books, and embellishments

Avery
www.avery.com
Labels and tags

Blue Cardigan Designs
www.bluecardigan.com
Unusual scrapbook papers

Clearsnap
www.clearsnap.com
Ink and rubber stamps

Crafters Pick
www.crafterspick.com
Ultimate glue

Creative Imagination
www.cigift.com
Scrapbook papers, supplies, and embellishments

Delta
www.deltacrafts.com
Acrylic paints and craft supplies

PAPER, PAINT, AND ART SUPPLIES

Dick Blick Art Materials
www.dickblick.com
Paper, paint, and art supplies

DMD Industries
www.dmdind.com
Corrugated paper

Dover Publications
www.doverpublications.com
Clip art, art stickers

EK Success
www.eksuccess.com
Scrapbook papers, supplies, and embellishments

Epson Co
www.epson.com
Photo and speciality papers

Family Treasures
www.familytreasures.com
Paper punches

Fancifuls, Inc.
www.fancifulsinc.com
Brass charms and embellishments

Fiskars
www.fiskars.com
Scissors and cutting implements

Foofala
www.foofala.com
Scrapbook and paper art embellishments

Glue Dots International
www.gluedotsinternational.com
Adhesive dots for paper craft applications

Golden
www.goldenpaints.com
Quality line of paints, fluid acrylics, and mediums for art

Grumbacher
www.grumbacherart.com
Paints and brushes

Headline
www.headlinesigns.com
Cardboard letter stencils

CRAFT SUPPLIES

Hobby Lobby
www.hobbylobby.com
Craft supplies

Ibico
www.ibico.com
Binding machines and supplies

Ikea
www.ikea.com
Fabrics and housewares

Jaquard
www.jacquardproducts.com
Artist paints and pearlescent powders

Jewelcraft
www.jewelcraft.biz
Embellishments including unique nailhead designs

Judikins
www.judikins.com
Stamps and supplies including Diamond Glaze

K & Co.
www.kandcompany.com
Scrapbook paper, albums, and embellishments

Kate's Paperie
www.katespaperie.com
Stationery, papers, and ribbon

Lasting Impressions
www.lastingimpressions.com
Brass templates and embossing supplies

Liquitex
www.liquitex.com
Paint and craft finishes

Making Memories
www.makingmemories.com
Scrapbook paper, tools, supplies, and embellishments

Martha Stewart Omnimedia
www.marthastewart.com
Home and craft supplies

Marvy Uchida
www.uchida.com
Markers and ink for paper crafting

May Arts
www.mayarts.com
Ribbons (wholesale only)

Michaels
www.michaels.com
Paper, paint, and art supplies

PAPER, PAINT, AND ART SUPPLIES

Midori
www.midoriribbon.com
Ribbon including printed varieties

National
www.natman.com
Hinges and hardware for unusual paper craft embellishments

Paper Parachute
www.paperparachute.com
Paper for paper art and scrapbooking

Paper Source
www.paper-source.com
Paper for paper art and scrapbooking

Plaid
www.plaidenterprises.com
Craft supplies including stamps, papers, and tools

PostModern Design
postmoderndesign@aol.com
Artstamps

Pressed Petals
www.pressedpetals.com
Pressed flowers for embellishments

Prism
www.prismpapers.com
Large selection of fine cardstocks for paper crafting including an exclusive textured line

Prismacolor
www.prismacolor.com
Colored pencils

Provocraft
www.provocraft.com
Coluzzle plastic template system

Prym-Dritz
www.prymdritz.com
Sewing notions and supplies

PSX
www.psxdesign.com
Artstamps and supplies

Quickutz
www.quickutz.com
Die-cut machine and unique alphabet and shaped dies

Ranger
www.rangerink.com
Rubber stamp and paper art inks and supplies

ReadySet
www.readysettools.com
Unique eyelet setting tool

Rollabind
www.rollabind.com
Binding machines and supplies

Rubber Stampede
www.rubberstampede.com
Artstamps

Sakura
www.sakura.com
Markers and pens

Sanford
www.sanford.com
Permanent markers

Sizzix
www.sizzix.com
Personal die-cutting machine

Stampendous
www.stampendous.com
Artstamps

Stampington and Co.
www.stampington.com
Rubber stamps, paper, and wire forms

Thermo Web
www.thermoweb.com
Click n Stick, adhesives

Tsukineko
www.tsukineko.com
Ink for rubber stamping and paper art

Uhu
www.uhu.de
Glue sticks and adhesive

U.S. ArtQuest
www.usartquest.com
Adhesives, paint, paper products

Victorian Trading Co.
www.victoriantradingco.com
Victorian goods for the home and crafter

The Vintage Workshop
www.thevintageworkshop.com
Vintage clip art and printable surfaces for fabric and paper arts

Walnut Hollow
www.walnuthollow.com
Wood embellishments and wood and paper burning tools for scrapbook and paper arts

Westrim
www.westrimcrafts.com
Scrapbook and paper art embellishments

Wordsworth
www.wordsworthstamps.com
Paper, stamps, and stencils for paper arts and scrapbooking

Wrights
www.wrights.com
Sewing trims

X-Acto
www.hunt-corp.com
X-Acto knives and blades

About the Author

Linda Blinn participates in the world of mixed-media art as an author, teacher, designer, and artist. She served on the editorial team of *Somerset Studio* magazine, *True Colors, Signatures,* and the *Art Journal Calendar,* published by Stampington & Co. As an editor, she focused on current trends in art journals, collage, magazines, and mixed-media art.

Her art has appeared in several magazines including *Victoria Magazine* and *Cloth, Paper, Scissors.* She has also been featured in *Artist's Workbooks and Journals* by Lynne Perrella; *Pockets, Pullouts, and Hiding Places* by Jenn Mason; and *Beyond Scrapbooks* by Barbara Bourassa.

She lives in the small coastal town of San Clemente, California, with her husband, Tom.

Her next books for Quarry are *Paper Studio Gifts* and *Paper Studio Baby,* coauthored with Jenn Mason and Jennifer Francis Bitto.

Acknowledgments

If I ever needed a reminder about having a supportive family, writing this book was it.

From proofreading to computer maintenance and just plain listening—Tom, Kari, Patrick, and Matthew—you are the best.

And grandkids, Katie and Case, thanks for helping me with our Ancestor Book and distracting me enough to remember to take you to the beach.

Jen and Jenn (Bitto and Mason), this roller coaster ride is much more fun with you two screaming in my ears. I promise you a lifetime of lemonade and Pinot Grigio… and double-sided tape.

And all of you talented and hilarious contributing artists—Lordy, girls, you knock my socks off. If I could only get all of you in the same room, we could tip the earth off its axis. Judy and Kelley, you went over top in talent, time, words, and generosity. In gratitude, I want to go to Paris with you and buy you the Eiffel tower.

And my girlfriends—you know who you are! Cheerleaders, wise women, givers, seekers, adventurers, warriors, comedians, and comrades. I want to grow old with all of you.

Linda